KITCHE

guide to

Divination

Finding, Crafting, and Using
Fortune-Telling Tools
From Around Your Home

PATRICIA TELESCO

New Page Books
A division of The Career Press, Inc.
Franklin Lakes, NJ

Copyright © 2004 by Patricia Telesco

KITCHEN WITCH'S GUIDE TO DIVINATION
EDITED AND TYPESET BY CLAYTON W. LEADBETTER
Cover design by Cheryl Cohan Finbow
Cover Illustration by Colleen Koziara
Printed in the U.S.A. by Book-mart Press

To order this title, please call toll-free 1-800-CAREER-1 (NJ and Canada: 201-848-0310) to order using VISA or MasterCard, or for further information on books from Career Press.

The Career Press, Inc., 3 Tice Road, PO Box 687, Franklin Lakes, NJ 07417
www.careerpress.com
www.newpagebooks.com

Library of Congress Cataloging-in-Publication Data
Telesco, Patricia, 1960-
  Kitchen witch's guide to divination : finding, crafting, and using
  fortune-telling tools from around your home / by Patricia Telesco.
    p. cm.
  Includes index.
  ISBN 1-56414-725-8 (pbk.)
    1. Divination. 2. Fortune-telling. I. Title.

BF1751.T46 2004
133.3--dc22

2004044823

Dedicated to the Hearth God
or Goddess in everyone!
Let's eat, drink, divine, and
make magick together.

Contents

Introduction 7

Part I
Scry If You Want to: The Art of Seeing 13

Chapter 1
What's Your Sign Baby?: Divination Basics 15

Chapter 2
Phone Home: Developing Your Inner Psychic ... 33

Chapter 3
Winging It: Choosing, Creating,
or Adapting Divination Methods 53

Part II
Multipedia of Kitchen Divination Methods 75

Chapter 4
Boards 77

Chapter 5
Candles 91

Chapter 6
Cards 99

Chapter 7
    Cast Systems 115

Chapter 8
    Coins 129

Chapter 9
    Dowsing 131

Chapter 10
    Drawn Systems 139

Chapter 11
    Dream Aids 147

Chapter 12
    Household Omens and Signs 153

Chapter 13
    Food Findings 157

Chapter 14
    Geomancy 173

Chapter 15
    Random Systems 177

Chapter 16
    Scrying 187

Chapter 17
    Helpful Hints 199

Appendix: Gods and Goddesses of Divination 205

Index 211

About the Author 217

Introduction

Let it be discovered by divination, or let a divinely inspired man declare it.

—Hittite prayer of Mursil II

How often have you heard yourself say, "I wish I had known ahead of time"? Well, count yourself in good company. Everyone wants a peek at the future, be it to see if that blind date's going to be a flop or fantastic, or to make a smart decision about an important career change. Truthfully, the nature of today's world is such that the only thing on which we can depend is change and the associated uncertainty it brings. The good news, however, is that there's a coping mechanism available—namely awakening and empowering your natural divinatory abilities so that you can get better perspectives on life's perplexities.

Before you get nervous, please know that I've been a kitchen witch for more than 20 years. During that time, I've discovered that magick and divination have very little to do with hocus-pocus, and a lot more to do with sacredness and spirituality. Everything in this book comes out of that experience, and centers on your personal space (especially the kitchen). Before you know it, you'll be in your pantry scrying with the best of them.

Certainly, this won't be like the tarot readers you've seen on TV, who overgeneralize and charge a fortune for their time. Instead, the focus here is on seeing yourself in a new way—as a person who can unlock the intuitive talents you have within, using things in and around your home, and then apply them proactively. (And all the better, that this isn't costly at all!). Instinct and intuition are certainly a natural part of human awareness. Additionally, psychic abilities are completely natural too. The only problem is that most people haven't been encouraged to develop them since youth. Thus, we turn to divination tools and methods to help us unlock those abilities and access information that eludes us in our busy day-to-day life. Early diviners played a role similar to modern counselors. Their task was to provide alternative perspectives and hope. Today, each of us is our own priest and priestess, counselor and guide. Anyone with the right intention and concentration can learn to make or adapt their own divination tools, then use them to gather the insights they most need—and that means *you*!

And you're certainly not alone. The interest in divination and fortune telling is growing steadily among people of all age groups and walks of life. Because it seems reason and religion are not always adequate for answering the questions that lay heavy on human minds and spirits, divination holds tremendous appeal. It offers anyone the gift of insight and a peek into realms often thought inaccessible. You want to know what's behind door number 2? Divination is one way to get those kinds of answers with a little training and tenacity.

Ah, but where to begin? Well, we can gather some hints from history. Divination is a time-honored tradition that appeared all over the world in many different forms. Because our ancestors had a very harsh life, they also had nagging questions and concerns about their fates. This, in turn, led to watching nature for omens and signs and creating a variety of predictive techniques, in an attempt to overcome fate's whims. No prophetic assistance that might prove helpful was overlooked. (Hey, I'm in this club too!)

Exactly how each divination method developed depended heavily on where and when it appeared. Divining by omens and signs was the first, quite simply because it required nothing more than keen observation skills. By 1400 B.C.E. healers in China were reading bones and shells to determine a patient's potential for recovery. Greek and Roman augurs listened to the wind and watched the birds for insights into the outcome of wars, and Tibetans used scrying to determine the Dali Lama's incarnations!

All of the people performing such arts provided a very valuable service to other individuals, communities, or whole countries. In the process, they also created a wonderful history upon which modern seekers can depend for tried-and-true divination methods to this very day. While society's perception of divination has been a love-hate relationship, depending on the era, the folk traditions from which many systems grew continued to thrive. Better still, for those of us who face hefty time constraints, many of these systems are wonderfully simple and pragmatic. *Kitchen Witch's Guide to Divination* was written with this tradition in mind.

Each of us faces a myriad of struggles daily. Divination is an instrument that helps us examine those issues objectively. To begin, however, each person has to understand what divination is and how it works (covered in Part I of this book). Building on that foundation, you also need to know how to choose or design divination systems successfully.

Following that path, *Kitchen Witch's Guide to Divination* goes on to examine some pantry-based, handy divination methods that are simple to learn and utilize, whether you're in your kitchen, back yard, office, or on the road. While I cannot begin to predict every question you might ask of such systems, I can help you learn about simple symbols that are around you every day and how to use them when your own perspective is lacking.

Divination opens a spiritual window to each person who ventures into its domain. Through these methods we can see our present situations more clearly and peek into future possibilities. In those moments when you find life moving too quickly, when situations seem chaotic and confusing, when you just need a different outlook or an advisor that requires nothing more than what you have at home, turn to this book as a helpmate. Then, create a pendulum, design a coupon tarot, carve some runes, light a candle, or roll the dice. Look at everything in your environment with new eyes, and trust the signs you receive. In the process, your understanding and appreciation of the simple truths evidenced in everything from the stars to the earth beneath your feet will grow proportionately—alongside your questing spirit.

Look up, look outward, look within.

Part 1

Scry If You Want to: The Art of Seeing

Welcome to the first part of your adventure. In this section of the book, we're going to focus on what farmers might call cultivating the soil (in this case, *spiritual* soil). More specifically, we'll examine common questions about divination and how it works, so you're more comfortable with whatever process you finally choose. We'll also talk about waking up your inner psychic so that those instincts respond naturally to any environment. Finally, we'll review effective ways to create or adapt divination systems so that, in the end, you'll have a wholly personalized system that's really right for your reality.

Chapter 1

What's Your Sign, Baby?: Divination Basics

*The future cannot be hidden or obscured
from the intelligent soul, but this perfect
knowledge cannot be acquired without
divine guidance.*

—Nostradamus

Before you go about trying various home divination systems, you probably have a dozen nagging questions about this ancient metaphysical art. A modern person's sense of logic and concrete thinking makes it difficult to accept the idea of personal revelation, especially with regard to the future. Rationality also tends to lead to natural doubts, which create a stumbling block to your eventual success. The purpose of this chapter is to help you overcome some of those hurdles by sharing insights to what a diviner has traditionally done, and how and why this information applies to you.

Along the way, you'll see a bit of history as that is our mirror. It reflects where we've come from so we can understand where our arts should be going in the future. It also provides important, time-honored constructs that have repeatedly proven successful for many people. With this understanding and information in hand, it makes it much easier to ponder what role divination should have in your life, and what system of divination is best for you personally.

20 Common Questions About Divination

It seems nearly every culture in every era had a means of trying to foretell the future. The fact that people continued to use those techniques means that a fair portion of the information received must have been valuable and viable. (Why use something if it doesn't work?) Indeed, in some cases such as that of a court astrologer or true seer, providing the wrong information could have meant his or her death. Nonetheless, these techniques cannot be proven 100-percent dependable. Rather, we have faith that they work. Bear this in mind as you read. Also please remember that what I'm providing here is a brief overview of a very diverse and sometimes complicated art. With that in mind, I've gathered comparative cultural studies of various divinatory methods and the ideals behind them, in hopes of providing you with a reasonably balanced and rational review of divination basics.

1. What does divination offer a person, both spiritually and mundanely?

It seems that most people go to a diviner to learn about future possibilities. After all, forewarned is forearmed! Consulting the cards, runes, or whatever system you choose (and getting their interpretive values) allows a person to examine potential opportunities or problems that didn't seem obvious through normal observations. If that same person has confidence in the information provided, he or she then can determine to make dynamic living changes to improve opportunities or offset those problems just around the corner.

However, I should note that the future isn't the only good reason to seek out a qualified reader. There are times when our present circumstances seem very confusing. No amount of thoughtful introspection seems to provide the perspectives we need. Divination tools and good readers can fill in some of those blanks with good advice!

While most people really know, deep down, what's best for them, reaching that information and obtaining a detached vantage point isn't easy. Using a personally devised or adapted divination system (or finding a reader) is another means to an end, and a holistic one at that. At its best, divination encourages us to step back, observe, ponder, discover, then finally act with wisdom as an ally.

2. Why are there so many different types of divination?

Each person is unique, and each of us relates to one of our senses most profoundly. I'm very tactile and love the feel of runes and stones. Highly visual people are drawn toward proverbial "eye candy," such as the tarot or animal cards. Thus it's not surprising that our ancestors devised a wide variety of divinatory methods to appeal to our natural need for sensory input.

More than this, however, divination tools reflect the immense diversity of the societies in which they originated. For example, in China the yarrow plant was highly respected both medicinally and symbolically. For a while the yarrow stalks were cast on the ground and the resulting patterns interpreted. It is from that simple approach that the I Ching system of divination eventually sprouted.

From a more historical vantage point, many divination systems often reflect our ancestors' lifestyles, which were often pressed for time, as are ours. Farmers, for example, would often observe the growth of specially planted crops for insights not only to the weather and crop cultivation, but also more personal questions. Likewise, a merchant heading out to trade might observe the stars for omens and signs in the hopes of improving sales, and traveling safely.

So basically people around the world have created divination systems that suited their living environment, era, and culture, often spontaneously. This is really the beauty of fortune-telling methods—they respond to individual vision and originality. Better still, this means that we have a long legacy of personally created divination systems on which to draw when devising our own meaningful approaches.

3. Is there anything that shouldn't be used for divination, and if so, why?

I'm of the opinion that our ancestors were highly pragmatic sorts. If something worked once, they used it again. If it worked more than once, it often became tradition, or minimally an ongoing personal practice. In other words, if they'd had lighters instead of matches, and microwaves instead of ovens, they would have probably found a way to integrate these items into spiritual pursuits.

As we look around the globe, there seems to be little (if anything) that people didn't use in an attempt to gain insights. Sticks, bones, clouds, wine, laughter, and even dirt were among the literally hundreds of methods we discovered. (It makes you wonder what that dust on the coffee table means!) Updating that a bit would imply that it's perfectly acceptable to look to our computers, TVs, cell phones, office supplies, and other modern symbolic items as potential oracular media or aids to creating one.

For example, I'm simply not an artist. (Most of my drawings could be done better by a 5 year old with crayons!) When I want to have special imagery for a unique form of cartomancy (divination with cards), I might photocopy the images desired and color them in. While it's not quite the same as creating the portraits from scratch, I still have to carefully consider which pictures best represent the meanings desired, as well as how to adorn each one. The *thoughtfulness* here is the key, not the *process*, per se.

Having said that, there is one caveat. As with all magick, the symbols or items chosen for a divination system *must* make sense to you and have a meaning to which you will easily relate when you use them. There probably never has been (nor ever will be) a system that appeals 100 percent to everyone, but if it's the system you're going to be using, it must appeal to your higher senses and connect intimately with your conscious and subconscious awareness. Otherwise it will be pretty much a waste of time.

4. Is it okay to adapt a divination system (that is, change it from the original form to something more personal)?

Absolutely. Begin, however, at the beginning. Get to know the system as it is and try to understand why the creator used the chosen symbols or components. Without that understanding it's going to be difficult to maintain continuity when you swap out items. Also, I'd give the divination system a little time to warm up before deciding to change it. Familiarity with a tool typically produces far better results. Because many prefabricated systems are quite costly, it would be a shame to alter it without a testing period first.

I would also add that it's important to be gentle in the way you transform a system. Some divination approaches have very long and well-respected cultural roots. We would not wish to offend a practitioner of a traditional system by adapting it, then still calling it by the same name, for example. If you change your tarot deck so it has no trump cards (kings, queens, and so on), then perhaps call it a neo-tarot. This indicates to anyone for whom you might read that you based your ideas on tarot, but have added your own personal changes so it functions better for you.

5. How can you tell what divinatory systems have merit?

Basically, you should evaluate by how well it works for you or the reader employing it. Unfortunately in the case of some divinatory tools like the Ouija, some of its functionality has been undermined by being classified as a "game." Effectively that removes the sacredness, and also the built-in protections that a wise reader utilizes (which is why you often hear about problems with Ouija boards).

Another thing that may limit the merit of a system is how one intends to apply it. For example a binary divination system like flipping a coin won't give you details or underlying energies in regard to a question. On the other hand, if all you want to know is *yes*, *no*, *stay*, *go*, and so forth, then it's perfectly suited to your needs. We need to look at both utility and effectiveness when judging the merits of a system.

6. Are divination tools treated like other magickal tools?

It has been my experience that most people who favor a specific divinatory tool treat it with some type of reverence. Why? Because it's always a good idea to respect the implements of your art so you don't misuse them. Just as a wood carver respects his or her knife's sharpness, respect toward your system honors the device's role in your spiritual life.

The way each person shows his or her respect varies. This reverence might mean the tool has a special box or pouch in which it's stored. Perhaps they leave it on the altar every day. Or perhaps they ask that no one else touch the tool. Why the request for no touching? Quite simply because the owner knows the more he or she handles a system, the more it's saturated with personal energy. In turn, this means the chosen system responds with greater accuracy for that individual.

As an aside, being protective of one's divination tool can often also protect a querent. Say someone unfamiliar with the tarot fiddles with a deck and pulls the Death card. That can scare the heck out of a novice who doesn't fully understand the card's meaning. So by maintaining control of his or her deck, the reader makes sure that they're present to explain the meanings in any spread.

By the way, cleansing tools after a reading is also common as it is with, say, an athame or chalice after a ritual. Whether the system gets smudged, sprinkled with lemon water, or held while the bearer visualizes white light doesn't matter—what matters is the grounding out of any residual energies left behind. This makes the tool fresh for the next reading. When this doesn't happen between readings, residual energy can skew the outcomes dramatically.

7. What about channeling and mediumship—are these types of divination too?

Consider for a moment that people came from miles around to consult the Oracle at Delphi in ancient Greece, believing that this woman was a direct channel for Apollo. Similarly, the Japanese had village oracles who were depended upon to share divine missives about upcoming rice harvests. These are but two examples where a specific spirit or deity was called into human form to gain access to important information for an individual or entire country. Because the word *oracle* means "to pray," the connection between individual and spirit(s) isn't surprising. The messages a person received from such individuals was pretty much the same as those provided by divination systems but for the additional element of having a helpful spirit, guide, or god. So, yes, this is a type of divination.

To understand the difference in processes, consider that your average tarot card reader does not give himself or herself to the cards. They simply interpret the outcome trusting on their intuitive instincts and psychic insights. By comparison, a medium or channeler *becomes* the oracle. It is not they who provide the information to a querent, but the spirit on whom they've called. For a moment in time, this individual becomes much like an interdimensional radio by adjusting to the frequency of that spirit, guide, or god, then broadcasting that message (hopefully without allowing personal ego or knowledge to taint what comes through).

That doesn't mean, however, that some diviners do not ask for divine assistance in their arts. In fact, the word *divination* implies that connection when translated from the Latin to mean "being in one condition with or from god." So the nonchanneler can certainly work cooperatively with sacred powers, the only difference here is that this person is not speaking *as* that power.

Also, I issue some caution about channeling, in that not all spirits have our best interests at heart. An experienced medium will immediately recognize a trickster spirit, while those less experienced may not. Any information obtained from such sources should be put in the skeptical review pile until you're certain it resonates with truth. This is good advice, actually, for any reading. Truth—if it is important to your life—will return again and again through unrelated sources so you can confirm its value.

8. Is there anything special that a person does to prepare before a reading?

Every person who works with divination systems often finds a miniritual of sorts that puts himself or herself in the right frame of mind and spirit. I personally like taking a bath with purifying herbs, followed by dabbing myself with oil of frankincense. Don't ask me why—it just helps. Other folks might light candles, burn incense, play soft music, or whatever. So you're likely to see a variety of preparation methods if you work with more than one reader.

This preparation time is very important, and if you begin doing a lot of readings you'll need to discover what sensual cues help you the most. Specifically you're looking for ways to put aside mundane thoughts and worries for a while and really focus on the tool you've chosen. Additionally you'll need to consider the question at hand, and how the symbols of your divination method relate to that question individually and as a whole. During this process, it helps to set aside personal knowledge and expectations so you don't accidentally skew a reading (positively or negatively). We'll be covering this in more detail in Chapter 2.

9. Should I voice my question to the reader or keep it to myself?

The answer to this question may be reader-dependent. Some people like to know the question so they can interpret the symbols with that question in mind. Other people prefer *not* to know the question so they don't go looking for information that isn't really presented by the symbols. Both approaches have merit.

The reader who asks what your question is will be able to give you more specific information because they have a frame of reference. The reader who does not know your question may end up being more generalized. On the other hand, they're also more likely to pick up subtle messages about which you *need* to know (versus wanting to know) because they have no idea what question you posed and aren't going to be swayed by that information. I tend to feel that the second approach is more objectified, but that doesn't mean the first approach is wrong or less useful. Much here depends on a reader's aptitude with his or her tools.

10. Does "god" provide the answers to readings or is there something else involved?

This is one of those loaded questions that depends, again, on faith. In the case of a medium or channeler, the belief is that this person's information comes from a spirit, guide, or god. In the case of a reader, this person's information comes from a blend of spiritual sensitivity and natural insights (and, of course, the symbols provided by his or her tools).

In general I think most diviners I've met see their work as a combined effort between self, psychic abilities, and the universe.

11. How much of a reading can I count on to be accurate, and if a reading is accurate, how does that happen?

Consider a reader as being analogous to a counselor. He or she is there to provide you with additional information, ideas, or insights you may not have had in making choices or considering a situation. Nonetheless, what you take away from this situation is up to you. Measure what you get against your spirit and heart. Take what helps, leave the rest aside. But if you go to several readers and hear the same thing over and over again, pay attention. Remember: A divination session won't always tell you what you want to hear, but rather what you *need* to know.

By the way, there are some warning signs that you're dealing with a reader whose motivations or methods may not be the best, or a reading that's somehow off the mark. These include:

- Any reading that leaves you feeling frightened or without choices.
- A reader who claims the information he or she gives you is 100-percent accurate.
- A reader or reading that instructs you to do something that goes against personal ethics or taboos.
- A reading that seems rushed, without any time to clarify or ask additional questions.
- A reading that lacks any specifics (overgeneralization is an old method used by "soothsayers"—they basically give the questioner just enough information to draw a conclusion, but it's nothing more than a psychological trick).

When any of the aforementioned happens in a reading, my best advice is to take what you get with a huge grain of salt. Know that even the best readers have "off" days, so don't necessarily assume you're dealing with a con artist or undertrained reader. However, if the same problems happen repeatedly with a diviner, I'd consider finding someone else to turn to for help (perhaps even *yourself*).

As for why you get accurate readings, especially about future matters, consider for a moment that humans are creatures of habit. We have very defined patterns in our lives, most of which do not change quickly. Also consider that every question we have in our minds and hearts bears a pattern. When we express that question, it appears in our aura. When we direct that pattern to the diviner and his or her tool, that pattern guides the results. You'll notice that nearly all divination systems require that you handle the tool in some manner (cut the cards, cast the stones, and so forth). That's so the pattern of your need/question can charge and change the tool's pattern, to evoke an informational response.

12. Will knowing my future change my future?

Ultimately a lot here depends on how you handle the information you're given. I have watched people return again and again to a wide variety of readers. Each one tells that person essentially the same thing—yet they continue asking the same question. This implies one of two things to me: Either that person isn't hearing what they want to hear, or they're very insecure and hope if they hear the same message often enough they'll finally act. Both implications aren't positive for those of us who strive to become our own priest, priestess, guide, and guru. Divination should never be used as a crutch or an excuse to procrastinate.

On the other hand, if the information you receive inspires you to think differently, act differently, to *do* something, then it will likely change the future. Time is a web. You cannot modify one strand without transforming the shape of others, hopefully in this case for the better!

13. Do you need to go to someone you know for a reading?

Not necessarily. In fact, some of the most amazing readings I've received were given by complete strangers. To explain: A friend or associate knows a bit about your life. This diviner might accidentally integrate what they know into a reading's interpretations (especially if the result of the reading seems very elusive).

Please know that this isn't a purposeful skewing. It's a natural filtering of information from the background of the reader's mind (the subconscious) to the conscious level, akin to what happens when you dream. Because the diviner is already in a receptive state of mind (as prepared for before the reading), that information can slip through without any real awareness of it. It's just part of human psychology. We're accustomed to hunting through mental files when an answer we seek to a question seems elusive.

A stranger, by comparison, knows nothing about your life or situation. They have no previous information on which to draw that could potentially taint a reading one way or the other. Divination involves a trinity of you, the reader, and the tool. When these interact, information comes forward. As mentioned earlier, the pattern of your question is the key to unlocking that information, so it doesn't really matter if you don't know the reader personally.

14. Are Internet readings viable?

Absolutely if performed by a reliable person. Similar to having a reading done by a stranger, this is just a stranger at a distance. When you e-mail this person, ponder your question and "send" the energy when you hit the send button. Energy is energy, and your computer works on electronics and phone lines, so there's no reason you can't use this bit of technology to transmit the pattern of your query to a long-distance reader. I've been doing readings over the Internet for several years and really find they're just as successful as in-person ones. In fact, in some ways they're better because the individual gets a typed review of the reading to which they can refer again and again for more insights.

15. Why do some readings seem to provide information for which you did not ask?

What we want and what we need is all to often two different things. A good reader knows this, and also knows that the pattern in your aura may express a *need*, not a want. Additionally, a reader who works cooperatively with the Divine may intercept messages from that source too. In either case, the reading is kind of like a living, fluid thing that can take very unexpected turns.

To give you a great example, I was reviewing a stone layout for a client and was very disturbed by what I saw in one part. It didn't seem to have anything to do with the rest of the reading, and I wondered if perhaps I'd screwed up somehow. Nonetheless the message was so intense, I chose to share it with her, with the understanding that I was a little uncomfortable by the lack of continuity in this part of the layout. Basically the stones indicated she was in some type of danger from a person walking a very fine mental line. Her reply to me was a very surprised "I've been being stalked. How did you know that?"

Now, I don't make it a habit to tell people things that alarm without also offering advice for how to make things better. When I asked if she'd gotten a restraining order, the thought hadn't occurred to her! So, in this instance, the information in the reading came forward in such a way to get this woman to act in her own best interest and really respect the potential dangers involved. (Sometimes we simply can't see things because we're so close to a situation.)

Another reason you might receive information you didn't request in a reading is simply because of random thoughts that wander through your mind while you're also thinking of your question. The human mind does hundreds of things at once, and rarely are we thinking of just one thing at a time. So while your question might be the foremost thought, divination tools may pick up this background noise and increase its volume by answering it in the reading. Typically when this happens, there's a very good reason. Something's sitting heavily in your subconscious and is trying to get your attention—so at least consider the message.

16. Why do some readers pull extra cards or stones at the end of a reading?

When I finish a reading there are times when it doesn't seem complete. I don't like leaving people without some sense of closure, so I'll have the questioner draw more stones or cards until that completion happens.

There are three other reasons why a reader might pull additional cards, stones, or whatever. First, if something seemed amiss in the reading (it lacked continuity), he or she may try to confirm what came forward. Second, if details were missing that the reader felt were important, he or she might want more symbols to clarify that issue. Third, if you're left with questions by the end of the reading (something which nearly all readers encourage to solidify the interpretive value in your own mind), the reader may pull more symbols to help in answering those questions, if the reading itself lacked the necessary details.

17. Do diviners have any ethical guidelines akin to what Witches have?

I've always been of the opinion that when one abuses spiritual aptitudes, one looses them. Nonetheless, there's no proverbial "10 Commandments" for diviners. That means that some folks you come across at, say, a psychic fair are likely just window dressing with no real ability. Others might have some ability but skewed motivations. So the key here is networking (word of mouth recommendations are best) to discover those readers whom others trust.

In particular you're looking for a diviner who will not read for someone if they have predisposed negative feelings toward a querent, or if they're feeling ill, out of sorts, or tired. You also want to seek readers who present bad news in positive ways (who leave you feeling hopeful and motivated). Other signs of an ethical reader include:

- ❧ He or she makes sure you won't be interrupted during your session.

- ❧ He or she offers a reasonable fee structure (including barter or trade).

- ❧ He or she takes time at the end of your session for questions or comments.

- ❧ He or she reminds you that the information obtained from readings is subjective, and that no divination system is 100-percent certain because of the human factors involved. You are always in the driver's seat with regard to your fate.

Finally, be aware that in some areas fortune telling is regulated. Some cities or counties outlaw it, others require a permit or license to practice, and others still require a sign saying "for amusement only." Ethical readers always mind the laws of the land, so knowing applicable laws in your area doesn't hurt.

18. Should I pay for my readings?

Sadly, I've found that people have more respect toward things for which they pay. Generally, compared to the freebie, people who pay for readings tend to be more attentive, take notes, and ask more questions (in an effort to get full value from their dollar).

On another level, readings require a lot of personal energy. When I've done 12 to 15 readings back-to-back throughout a day, I'm exhausted afterward. In the mundane world, we pay people to "work" (expend personal energy), and this is really no different. We also pay counselors and psychologists. (And trust me when I say a divinatory reading is far less expensive!)

Charging a reasonable sum for one's readings keeps people from randomly volunteering the diviner's abilities as if they were a sideshow act. Some folks use the money they make to help supplement family income. In any case, most ethical readers will suggest viable alternatives to cash if you're really in need of assistance. Spiritual knowledge should not be limited by the size of one's pocketbook, and there are certainly other ways to honor a reader's time and energy than simply cash. Offer to do a chore, exchange readings with that person, or perhaps you have a craft that you could barter. I think you'll discover this approach is highly respected in many New Age venues.

On the other hand, please think truthfully about the level of your financial need before you ask about barter or sliding scale fees. I have watched people walk away from a reader after having negotiated a lower rate, and subsequently spend $300 on a robe or athame without haggling a bit. That left the reader pretty upset when she found out (and for good reason). Abusing the good-hearted nature of the Neo-Pagan community isn't wise if one ever hopes to receive it again. Honesty is always the best policy.

19. How often should I have a reading done for myself?

Kind of like spiritual medication, have a reading done only when you feel you really need insight that you can't get from normal sources. It's not healthy to utilize divination systems for every question or situation; that makes it a crutch instead of a tool. It cheats a person out of the learning experience that comes from making choices and mistakes without something external to credit or blame.

You—not your psychic—are responsible for your life and what you make of it. Yes, periodic readings can really help put a new spin on things. And learning to read for yourself will become a fun, and functional way of expanding your spiritual horizons. Nonetheless, treat it respectfully. When you honor something, you're less likely to misuse it in your life or anyone else's.

20. Can anyone learn to read for himself or herself?

Absolutely. In fact, that's part of what this book is all about. Each person has some level of natural psychic aptitude. It just takes a little time and training to open the inner doorways so your talent gets activated more regularly. With patience, practice, and persistence, your level of success will steadily grow, especially when you find or make just the right divination system for yourself.

While there was a time when divination was kept in the hands of Shamans, priests, and priestesses, one of the goals of the New Age movement is reclaiming that role in our lives. The diviner's art is part of that, as it encourages and fulfills that connection between self and spirit so we can see our todays more clearly and peek toward the tomorrows with hopefulness.

Chapter 2

Phone Home:
Developing Your Inner Psychic

*He who controls the past commands the
future. He who commands the future
conquers the past.*

—George Orwell

With the main questions and concerns tackled, now
the question becomes one of activating the inner psychic so
you don't always have to depend on a reader for assistance.
At least one hurdle most people face in this process is
realizing and accepting that you (yes, *you*) are a magickal,
spiritual being and have all the potential necessary to per-
form divination. This isn't a clique or club—it's a part of
human nature that we've shoved into a corner because it
can't be easily qualified or quantified. Well, it's long past
time to dust off the cobwebs and allow yourself to become all you can be, mentally and psychically. I combine
these two because I honestly see psychism as a gift of
the mind. We have only begun to discover the mind's
wonders, and there is so much more about which we do
not understand. I believe, as do many other people, that
psychic abilities fall into this uncharted territory.

Throughout time, seers, kings, and commoners alike have tried various methods for awakening these gifts. A fair number of these techniques are still used today to improve the flow of spiritual energy and bring a person's conscious awareness to higher, more receptive levels. The ones you'll learn about in this chapter will be:

- ✍ Meditation and visualization.
- ✍ Chanting, prayer, or mantras.
- ✍ Cleansing and purification.
- ✍ Rituals or spells.

To this foundation, we'll also review how ambiance, timing, and other little "touches" can really make or break a divinatory effort. The most important thing you can bring to your reading at this juncture, however, is patience. No one learns to be an adept diviner over night. It may take you months or years to perfect your art. But as my mother used to say, anything worth doing is worth doing well. That means taking your time and working at a pace that's right for you.

History of Psychism

Let me back up for just one moment and assure you that you are not alone in trying to discover and empower your inner psychic abilities. Some of the greatest minds throughout humankind's history mused over our potential spiritual powers, especially those things not easily explained. For example, the Syrian philosopher Posidonius believed that divination and visions depended on the action of daemons that communicated to humans through a kind of telepathy. Juvenal (a Roman poet) wrote about how the Chaldean women not only asked fortune tellers about the future, but then took steps to influence that future.

While some folks wrote about divination, others were finding new and unique ways of employing it. In Babylon, there were sky omen interpreters, who likely helped popularize astrology. Of course various prophets were all the rage in the ancient world. In Greece, people went before statues of Hermes, whispered questions to him, then went outside to wait for the first phrase they heard. This phrase was their answer!

What about other media used for divination? Well, here are a few somewhat unusual examples and their origins:

- ১১ Aprons (Victorian American).
- ১১ Arrows (Korean).
- ১১ Axe (Hebrew and Greek).
- ১১ Bamboo sticks (Chinese).
- ১১ Beans (European).
- ১১ Boards (Tanzanian).
- ১১ Bread (Italian).
- ১১ Bulls (Celtic).
- ১১ Cheese (Greek and Roman).
- ১১ Coconut (African).
- ১১ Drums (Siberian).
- ১১ Fans (Surinamese).
- ১১ Horses (German).
- ১১ Masks (Mayan).
- ১১ Needles (Cherokee).
- ১১ Onions (German).
- ১১ Popcorn (Navaho).
- ১১ Rice (Chinese).
- ১১ Roses (Greek).
- ১১ Scarves (Tibetan).
- ১১ Thunder (Egyptian).
- ১১ Tops (Siamese).

- ౨ Twitching (New Zealand).
- ౨ Wheel (Asia Minor).
- ౨ Wood (Scandinavian).
- ౨ Wreath (German).

The interest in divination certainly doesn't end there. In more recent times, the term *psychical research* first appeared in 1882, through the Society of Psychical Research in England. Two years later it spread to the United States, Germany, Russia, France, Holland, and other countries. In 1969, the Parapsychological Association joined the American Association for the Advancement of Science in the United States. In 1972, the International Congress of Psychologists, held in Tokyo, Japan, heard reports on parapsychology from the Soviets and foreign scientists.

American astronaut, Edgar Mitchell, held telepathic experiments between Earth and Apollo 14. He wrote, "For mankind, these experiments may be more significant than space research itself." Alongside such notable individuals as Mr. Mitchell, institutions such as the John F. Kennedy University and the University of Iceland have special departments dedicated to psychic research and related mental aptitudes. This is no longer the realm of the mad man...yesterday's magick is becoming today's science!

Where Is This "Inner Psychic" Hiding?

Since we were very young, people have been telling us "it's just your imagination" when it comes to any type of paranormal or supernatural experience. Unfortunately, when we hear something enough, we begin to believe it. So over time, many of us naturally pushed down those instincts and abilities, not wishing to be laughed at or tossed in a loony bin. To dig them out, we need to start at the beginning.

Think back to when you were younger. Do you remember those moments when you just *knew* your best
friend was thinking about you, or when you seemed in-
nately aware that the phone was about to ring? These are
two examples of your inner psychic trying to break loose.

Typically, even with societal bulldozing, most of us
still have these kinds of experiences. For example, just the
other day I got up and walked to the front door and
grabbed the knob before the bell rang. This startled me,
and I stopped to ask my husband if what I thought just
happened, had indeed happened! In retrospect, I was a
tad annoyed at myself for not trusting what my eyes and
body were obviously telling me. Yet I'm not alone in that
kind of reaction. I'm just like thousands of other people
who are still struggling with their ability to tap the higher
self and Spirit for improved insights.

So, how do we overcome this insecurity and begin the
lesson in trusting? Well, divination tools are at least part of
the answer. Focusing on tools lets us direct our attention
somewhere other than the self. We can see and touch the
symbols before us, and read them like the page of a book.
This seems much easier than drawing all that information
out of ourselves. What we don't realize is that the process
hasn't changed at all—you just have a helpmate in gathering that information and making it clear!

No need to stop there, however. There are numerous
techniques that spiritual people around the world have utilized to help them release the mundane world and touch
eternity. It may take some experimentation on your part
to discern which techniques are going to be most helpful
to opening your psychic doorways. I do suggest trying all
of these methods a couple of times and making notes as to
whether your divinatory efforts afterward seemed to improve or not. Why try more than once? Because any number of external and internal factors can influence the

effectiveness of a spiritual methodology. Perhaps you're tired...or maybe the phone rings in the middle of your pre-divinatory meditation. That kind of distraction usually leads to not achieving the deep, altered state of awareness for which you hoped (and that, in turn, affects how accurately you interpret the symbols in a reading).

Mindful Meditations and Visualizations

Meditation is a wonderful technique that helps us alleviate mundane stress and refocus our awareness toward more spiritual matters. It's been proven that a person who meditates regularly experiences improved health and decreased anxiety-related disorders. Removing that kind of negative energy from your aura also naturally improves the flow of spiritual energy, which you can, in turn, direct toward divinatory efforts.

The difficulty many people have with meditation is that they find it hard to "turn off" all the noise in their minds. This is perfectly normal and shouldn't deter you from trying, as meditation gets easier with practice. In fact, you probably meditate already without even knowing it. Ever get so enthralled with a book or a project that you don't even notice when someone else enters the room? That's a kind of meditation! So, you'll know you're doing it right when you have a similar experience without the external focal point.

I've found that meditation is helped greatly by breathing slowly and evenly. Close your eyes and direct your attention to your heartbeat and every breath you take. Now consciously slow things down just a bit. Breathe in through your nose and out through your mouth, at a metered pace. Allow the last breath to connect to the next. Feel your muscles begin to relax and your mind clear of clutter. That's how you should be when you try any divination effort. See, the idea behind meditating before divination is that of focusing on the task at hand, releasing the tensions that could hinder your efforts, and generally moving into a spiritual state of awareness that's open to receiving input.

In combination with breathing, various visualizations may help you open your psychic centers. If, for example, you're planning to work with Deity as a guide in a reading, you could visualize your crown chakra opening. Visualize this as a spiral of energy (turning to the left to open, right to close). Alternatively to open your intuitive abilities, visualize the third eye chakra (located central to your forehead), spiraling counterclockwise as it expands to receive information.

Sometimes I visualize a yellow-gold light flowing through me while I breathe. This hue is attuned to divinatory and psychic energies. It's also a communicative color, which helps you better interpret symbolic language. Give it a try and see how you feel afterward. Other ideas include wearing a yellow shirt while you're doing a reading, burning a yellow candle, and so on. You may also find that playing relaxing music is helpful to your meditation efforts. My best advice is to try a variety of sensual activities (mixing and matching) until you find the one(s) that work best for you.

Another piece of advice is to start out slowly. Try meditating at first, for just a few minutes. (Trust me when I say if you've never done this before even 5 minutes seems to be an eternity.) Novice meditators often find that their nose itches, or a particular muscle twitches. This, again, is due to your mind looking for more input (the noise it's used to). You need to get past those points. Once you do, start increasing the amount of time you meditate. Even 15 minutes daily, especially before you try divination, will prove very beneficial, both spiritually and mundanely.

Vocalizations

Words have power. When you speak specific words in specific combinations they convey specific meanings to those listening. The words also bear vibrations that transform the air around the speaker. The more charged those words are, the more active the air becomes. To see a good example of this in action, watch any sports event where people are cheering. The excited energy become contagious and spreads outward.

Putting this into a magickal construct, prayers, chants, mantras, and affirmations are one way that we can reattune our auric envelope to harmonize with the frequencies of not only our question, but also Spirit. Let's look at each of these individually.

Prayer implies working with Deity, so it would be most effective for someone who plans to ask for divine assistance in his or her reading. Prayer has many more dimensions to it, however. It's a means of saying thanks, and also of just talking to Spirit. A person who is prayerful bridges the gap between the temporal and astral using prayer to fulfill his or her role as a *walker between the worlds*. After all, isn't that what a diviner is truly doing—going from one state of awareness to another and gathering information along the way?

The main difference between prayers and chants is two-fold. Chants may, or may not be aimed at Deity. Rather the words are carefully chosen for their vibrational affect on the aura. Also, chants are repetitive, the belief being that not only does the repeated sound reshape the auric envelope, but hearing it helps the chanter move into a trans-like state from which it's easier to interpret a reading with clarity. One of the most commonly known chants is *om*, meaning simply "I am." Om affirms the self and the spiritual nature, and it's a perfectly good chant to try before divination.

By the way, chants need not always be spoken—sometimes they're sung. In a group setting this makes for a beautiful blend of individuality with the harmony of a common goal and mingling energies. You don't need to be a great singer either. (Hey, if you're working alone, your only "critic" is you or Spirit, and I'm quite sure the Divine is more concerned with intention than being on key!)

Mantras tie into chants in that they're (by definition) Vedic chants. However, in New Age ideology, the word *mantra* has slightly different connotations. Some people believe that each person has a mantra—a combination of words or sounds that can help in the pursuit of enlightenment (and in our case, divinatory efforts). I found this out quite by happenstance during a group meditation, wherein a series of words came into my mind. Speaking them out loud seemed to fill the air around me with a nearly visible shimmer and shift of energy. I asked the group leader about it, and he explained about the personal mantra theory. Because I'm not a huge advocate of speaking in other languages unless you're very familiar with both pronunciation and meaning (such as the Vedic texts), the personal mantra offers an alternative for your consideration.

How do you discover these words? Try a prayer or meditation (or both), in which you ask for guidance and power words. If you begin getting those words, write them down and speak them slowly and rhythmically. As you listen to your voice, make note of how you feel. Typically a good personal mantra leaves the skin somewhat tingly. It raises your energy, improves your ability to center and focus, and helps activate your psychic centers. Thus, when you find one, it's perfectly apt to utilize it as part of your divination efforts.

As an aside, I recognize that there will be times when you cannot vocalize a prayer, chant, or mantra. In such instances, it's wholly acceptable to *think* the words instead. Remember that thoughts are simply words uttered inwardly. As long as you approach those thoughts with the same respect as you do the sacred vocalizations, they can have an equal affect on your aura and efforts.

Squeaky-Clean Clairvoyance

In many ancient settings, it was considered unseemly to go before the sacred powers without some type of bathing or other personal preparations. I believe that divination methods direct sacred energies into an answer, so I feel that we should likewise prepare ahead of time for the task. Even as one might take a ritual bath before going to Circle, the idea here is to proverbially polish up your aura so it has no residual energies that could hinder a reading.

As with many things along a rather eclectic spiritual path, cleansing and personal preparations take many forms. The bath I just mentioned is certainly one of them, as is hanging some cleansing herbs in the shower (as the hot water hits these, they release purifying aromas). Other people may simply rinse their hands in rose or lemon water, and smudge their divinatory tools with sage. Others still might use prayer, meditation, and/or visualization to direct cleansing energy throughout the auric envelope. I encourage you to try a couple of these approaches to see which one leaves you feeling "squeaky clean," in the spiritual sense.

This is also a good chance to do a quick personal check. What is your state of mind and body? Are you tired? Angry? Ill? Out of sorts? Those types of energy drains will negatively impact any divinatory effort. You're better off to wait until body, mind, and spirit are all on a positive wavelength.

Last, but certainly not least, just before you begin a reading, stop for a moment. Breathe deeply. Perhaps invoke the aid of guides or Spirit. Ask yourself if your motivations are sincere and guided by desiring the greatest good. This last moment is very important as it sets the tone for the interpretation phase of the effort. In a way, this brief waylay becomes like a miniritual that puts you in the best possible frame of mind for approaching your divination tools. It reminds you of the sacred energies and responsibilities involved.

Empowering Spells and Rituals

Just because divination is a metaphysical process doesn't mean that it can't benefit from the energy of spells and rituals. In fact, the symmetry of energies should improve your results, if you've been having difficulty. In designing your spells or rituals, however, it helps to know about some of the components that support the goal of psychic sensitivity. Among those that were used traditionally, we find this sampling:

- Amethyst.
- Azurite.
- Broom.
- Cherry.
- Citrine.
- Dandelion.
- Fig.
- Hazel.
- Holey stone.
- Jet.
- Lapis.
- Moonstone.
- The number 5.
- Obsidian.
- Orange.
- Pomegranate.
- Quartz.
- Rowan.
- Tiger's eye.
- Yellow items.

These components can be assembled any number of ways. For example, you could light five yellow candles and burn some orange incense as part of a spell, adding an invocation such as:

> With the light of one, this spell's begun;
> With the light of two, my vision–true;
> With the light of three–bring insight to me;
> With the light of four–mystical energy outpour;
> With the light of five–the magick's alive!

Leave the candles and incense burning while you work with your divinatory tools.

Let's consider another example. Say that you're working on creating a dream catcher (see page 149). You could consider integrating some of these components (like amethyst beads and tiny rowan twigs ornamentally assembled on a yellow base). While you're applying the various elements to the base material, add an incantation such as:

> Bring me visions and spiritual dreams;
> Come through the starlight, carried on moonbeams;
> Bring me dreams while here I lay,
> And hold the memory close come the break of day.

Make sure to hang the dream catcher near your bed, and have a pen or tape recorder handy for whatever dream-time memories with which you wake.

Another way to utilize spellcraft or miniritual components is by blessing and energizing the divination medium for the task ahead. Say, for example, you plan to use a particular herb for a pendulum (see page 135). A short, focused incantation or prayer helps designate the component for specific energies, and also eliminates any unwanted energy from the equation. In this case you might say something such as:

Blessed by Spirit, burning bright,
Energized for clear insight,
My will directed, focused energy sent,
Saturate this herb with discernment.

If you wish, you can repeat this or any other incantation while you're utilizing your chosen components for the reading.

But what about rituals? While you can certainly enact any of these spells in a longer, ritualized format, I think there's a better way to utilize ritual for divination—namely that of setting sacred space. Because there's going to be many occasions during which you can't enact a full formal ritual before doing a reading (hey, our lives are pretty hectic), the alternative is creating a protected region in which your reading won't be deterred by unwanted energies. Additionally, during the creation of sacred space you can invoke the assistance of a deity or spirit guide if you so choose (For your reference, a discussion of various divinatory deities is provided in the appendix on page 205).

For those readers who may be unfamiliar with the idea of sacred space, the basic concept is that of making a temporary sphere of energy guarded by Elemental energy around the region in which you're planning to work. This sphere keeps the desired psychic vibrations inside, and outside interference neatly *out*! The only exception is if you invite Deity or a spirit guide, in which case that presence remains with you until you dismiss the space.

Most Witches begin creating sacred space in the East (where the sun rises), moving clockwise around the circle, stopping in the South, West, and North to welcome the Powers, and finally end in the center to honor Spirit. I feel this is an ideal configuration for divination because this psychic aptitude is associated with the East, insight, and communication! However, if the topic of your divination efforts seems more aligned to a specific Element (such as money matters tying into the Earth Element), you might consider starting the invocation process at that quarter to honor those energies first. This is really a personal decision, not one of protocol.

Speaking of the invocation—before that word makes you antsy, know that it simply means "invite." You are not commanding the Elements or spiritual beings, you're inviting their aid. And thankfully for us, the Powers are generally responsive to respectful, honest inquiries!

As to the wording of an invocation, it need not be fancy or flowery—just meaningful! In particular, use words with which you're comfortable and that indicate the purpose for calling on these Powers (namely the divination effort you'll be enacting while in the sacred space). Here's one example with which you can tinker to your heart's content:

Guardians of the East, Power of Air,
I call and welcome you to protect this sacred space.
Bear on your winds fresh insight;
Let the light of dawn shine upon me,
Enabling me to see meanings clearly.

Guardians of the South, Power of Fire,
I call and welcome you to protect this sacred space.
Bear on your sparks the warmth of good intentions;
Let your embers spark my inner hearth,
To burn with even mindedness.

Guardians of the West, Power of Water,
I call and welcome you to protect this sacred space.
Bear on your waves healthy inspiration;
Let your mists settle gently,
To quench my questing spirit.

Guardians of the North, Power of Earth,
I call and welcome you to protect this sacred space.
Bear in your soils spiritual enrichment;
Let your loam be rich,
To nurture my soul and answer it's questions.

So be it!

NOTE: If you're welcoming a deity or spirit guide, it would be done in the center of your sacred space with suitable words that follow a pattern similar to the rest of your invocation. It's also nice to light a candle here, which not only represents the Powers, but also your own spirit's interaction in this process.

At this juncture get comfortable and proceed with your reading. Don't forget to take notes so you can ponder meanings in the days and weeks ahead. Last but not least, release the sacred space by thanking the Powers for their presence and help, and letting them go on their way. Again this need not be complex. You can say something such as:

Powers of Earth, thank you for your presence and help.
Please carry the sacred energies with you
across the land as you leave this space.

Merry Part!

NOTE: I used the example of Earth, because many people like to dismiss the quarters in reverse order (counterclockwise) to symbolically unwind the energy.

Other Helps and Hints

If you've tried the ideas in this chapter and still find you're having trouble getting accurate readings, don't despair. There can be any number of reasons for your difficulties, including the setting in which you enact a reading, and even possibly having chosen the wrong divination tool for yourself. We'll be talking about choosing, adapting, and making tools in the next chapter, but here let's look at some other potential factors.

First there's timing. While this isn't a *must*, a lot of ancient Mages depended on auspicious timing for enacting spells, rituals, and prognostications. I see no reason not to try this yourself, if practicable. Here's a list of various timing considerations that you might apply to divination efforts:

- **Monday:** Named after the moon, this day inspires intuitive skills.
- **Tuesday:** Take a look at your reading on a Tuesday if you want a more rational outlook.
- **Wednesday:** Inspires mystical energy.
- **Saturday:** The day of outcomes and understanding cause and affect, working this day should improve your overall comprehension of a reading.
- **Midnight:** The witching hour during which the veils between the worlds are said to grow thin (this is also true of New Year's holidays such as Samhain).
- **April:** A month focused on "fate," most divinatory efforts should improve during this month because the path is more "open" then.
- **September:** A time to begin grasping the deeper meanings in some of your readings that previously eluded you. Go read them again!
- **November:** A good month for overall psychic development and energy.
- **Full Moon:** For "fullness" in your visionary perspectives.

- **Moon in Aries:** Good for developing your skill with a specific media.
- **Moon in Cancer:** Strong lunar energies for creative interpretations.
- **Moon in Libra:** For balanced discernment.
- **Moon in Pisces:** Overall intuitive, spiritual energy.

I have said many times that I feel *anytime* is the right time for magick, if you have the proper focus and motivations. The addition of special timing simply supports your goal(s), thereby improving results.

The next helpmate is ambiance, or in current terminology: *location, location, location!* While you might not think about it much, where you're enacting a reading and the overall atmosphere in that region can dramatically affect your accuracy. For example, I find most people have trouble doing anything in the bedroom other than dream-work because it doesn't inspire energy—it inspires napping! Similarly I had difficulty using my office for the longest time because it originally was a nursery for one of our children. I'd forgotten to cleanse and adjust the energies after we moved the furniture around, but the mommy in me still thought of the room as baby's space!

So in considering ambiance, look at both obvious and subtle things that may be affecting you or the energy in your oracle. For example, is the phone turned off? Is there too much fluorescent light (which speaks of the conscious, logical mind, not the intuitive nature)? Is there too much noise to focus on your question or to interpret the reading without distraction? In my case, I like to straighten the area in which I'm working because I find clutter makes my mind wander toward mundane thoughts (mostly of cleaning).

After you've done a quick review for these types of issues, the next step is thinking about the kinds of things you could add to your surroundings to help put you in the best frame of mind. Here are some ideas to consider:

- Light a candle to encourage a meditative state of mind (a yellow candle is a good choice, as yellow represents the psychic self).

- Play specially chosen music (I recommend something without words, as the lyrics of a song can get stuck in your head and end up in the reading).

- Burn incense that heightens your spiritual and psychic awareness (lotus and sandalwood are both good choices).

- Dim the lights a little (add more candles if need be). As mentioned before, psychologically most people unconsciously associate lights with daily, mundane activities.

- Wear comfortable clothing that won't distract you while you're sitting and mulling over the results.

Please remember that the failure of a reading to answer your question or accurately predict the future does not mean total failure on your part or that of the divination medium. There are times when the answer I get is "things are just too messy right now to clarify." Yeah, I know...not exactly helpful...or is it? Sometimes we are so close to a situation that we don't realize the chaos going on or we'd take whatever reading we got and interpret it incorrectly because of our lack of perspective.

This brings me to an important point—your perspective matters! The energy in your aura at the time of a reading matters! If you're confused, the reading may come out sounding very confusing. Similarly, if you're angry, it's likely to come out with darker energies. So take into account the ambiance you carry with you all the time when considering the success or failure of an effort. And, by the way, it's perfectly okay to repeat a reading if it comes out oddly. You can try right away or in a day or two, with the same question. The second reading may clarify, confirm, or deny the first by its outcome.

Why would you get two readings about the same question with different answers? Because you either did something to change your fate, or one of the readings was inaccurate (for any of the possible reasons we've already discussed). To know for sure, try a tie breaker! They say "three is a charm."

Lastly, if I could leave you with one final piece of advice when it comes to psychic information and divination, it would be simply: sometimes a rock is just a rock. Not everything in life *has* to have intense spiritual significance. A situation in your life could be just normal life happening! I've often joked with folks about creating a system based on various body odors just for the fun of it. You laugh, but unfortunately some people get so caught up in their yearning for spiritual experiences that they forget to keep one foot on the ground, and actually seem to look for signs everywhere. No one needs omens, signs, portents, and divinations to know how to run every moment of every day. Just live it! Be the magick, and on those days when you get stuck with really difficult questions, then consider divination as an ally.

Chapter 3

Winging It: Choosing, Creating, or Adapting Divination Methods

And the many ways of prophesy I put in order.

—Aeschylus

Before we talk about adapting or creating a divination system, let's talk about what makes for a good tool for your personal use. Go shopping at any New Age store and you're likely to find everything from angel cards and pendulums to dousing rods and runes. Now, none of these items is what one might call "cheap," so you don't want to buy without some serious thought as to whether or not this system will work for your needs and goals.

The first bit of advice I give people is to think about the sense to which you respond most strongly. If you're a highly tactile person, you'll probably enjoy stones or runes much more than tarot cards. On the other hand, runes don't offer the same type of information and only have 21 symbols, as opposed to 72 in the tarot. As you can see, this is where things start to get a bit complicated.

Pendulums and dousing rods help locate things. The pendulum's motions can also be observed to obtain the answers to questions. However, whether it's swinging left and right, forward and backward, or kitty-corner is not only a bit subjective, depending on your vantage point, but can also be influenced by many factors (not the least of which is someone bumping the table accidentally). So these wonderfully sturdy systems also have some limitations of which you need to be aware before buying.

For visually oriented people, the tarot (or variations thereto) seems to be the most popular divination tool because it offers a depth of interpretive values. Thanks to creative artists, there are literally thousands of styles and themes from which to choose. On the down side, tarot cards are not very forgiving of coffee or tea stains, they don't hold up well to frequent handling, and 72 symbols and their interactions aren't easy to memorize.

It's not lazy to consider the divination system's level of difficulty as a factor in your decision-making process (namely how long it will take before you become proficient). As a beginner, it's often easier to have a tool with fewer symbols because you'll be able to remember the meanings more quickly. There's nothing that tends to disrupt a reading more than having to flip through pages of a book to figure out interpretive values!

Another factor in your decision, of course, is how you respond to the entire system on a spiritual level. Extend your senses. Look, touch, sense! Take a deep breath and consider how the medium comes across. Is it warm and welcoming, or does it feel like static? The first is a positive sign, the second negative. Note, however, that your reaction to a system may come through a sense other than touch. Ponder smells, tastes, or sounds that occur while you're examining the media too (most people get messages through the sense to which you most strongly respond naturally).

If you choose tarot as your tool, it's in your best interest to go to a store with a large variety of opened decks that you can look through. The cover of a box and the few images on the back are simply not enough from which to make an informed choice. I'm speaking from experience here in that I saw a deck whose imagery on the box was simply stunning. Sadly, the rest of the deck did not meet that standard when I opened them. Once opened, however, a deck can't be returned to the store unless the owner is willing to utilize it as a sample. Thus, my advice regarding looking through as many opened samples as possible before making a purchase.

If you don't happen to live in an area with a store that has opened divination systems for you to try out—ask your friends for recommendations or check online for more details (especially reviews). Thankfully Websites such as *www.amazon.com* often post a fair variety of images and samples from the instructional material. This isn't a perfect solution, but it's a lot better than buying wholly sight-unseen.

Steps for Choosing a Divination System

1. Review the systems that appeal to you.
2. Narrow down those systems to no more than 3 to 5 choices.
3. Appraise the difficulty of the systems.
4. Appraise the functionality of the system considering your lifestyle.
5. Start considering your order of preference; do not rush.
6. Feel out the systems and how your higher senses respond to each.

7. Obtain or make the media for your final choice.

8. Give the system a six-month trial period.

9. Allow for changes in media when you experience dramatic transformations.

Please take your time in making this choice. Do your research. Learn about what types of symbols and systems seem to inspire you the most. While it's very exciting to obtain your first divination tool, that excitement will fade quickly if it's not what you hoped. In fact, I've seen people give up trying altogether because a system left them so terribly wanting. This is a shame, as divination can be a wonderful spiritual helpmate. Rather than find you among those disappointed folk, I'd rather advise a slow, steady decision-making process in the hope that your final choice is not only "right" but also very inspirational.

Once you get your medium home, give it at least six months as a trial period. It often takes at least three just to get comfortable with the energies of a system, and become familiar with the symbols. The next three months allow you to test your overall level of satisfaction with the media and its accuracy on yourself, friends, and associates alike.

By the way, this whole process works well should you someday find that your tried-and-true divination system gets stale. When we go through various personal and spiritual changes, our tastes in divination systems may also change (let alone what we need them to do). So be aware of this possibility, and keep your eyes and options open. There's no need to "marry" yourself to one method (in fact, many people have more than one, each of which has a specific function).

Adapting A Prefabricated System

As humans, being somewhat persnickety, we often find a divination system that we like for the most part, but that also seems to have limitations or symbols to which we can't seem to relate well. Now what? You've already spent the money. You've already learned the basics. Well, how about tweaking the system to better meet your needs? No, this is not disrespectful—it's simply a very logical solution to the problem at hand.

How do you go about making adaptations? First look at the base media. If you're going to add new symbols to a set of runes, for example, you'll want the same type of stones as your original ones. This helps the grouping maintain a continuity of energy (in other words, the runes are more likely to work cooperatively). Once you have the foundation, you can carve or paint it as desired.

What about choosing the additional emblems? The best approach is to ask yourself what you feel the current system is missing, then find representations that provide that missing element. For example, runes don't really have symbols for people like the tarot does, so perhaps you could create a stone for *man, woman,* and *child.* In this case a phallic symbol, yoni, and seed might work to represent those energies. Determine (in detail) what each new symbol will mean alone or in combination with the rest of the set. Write down this information and keep it with your interpretation booklet.

Other systems require different approaches. For the tarot, I suggest buying a blank deck of cards the same size as the deck you currently own. It's vital that the cards are the same size so that you can't inadvertently skew a reading by pulling the odd-card(s). Draw your new symbols and imagery on these cards and gently spray the surface with a fixative so it won't easily smudge (ask your local art store what they suggest depending on whether your image is in pencil, crayon, pastel, or paint).

The most important factors for adding in new symbols to any system are:

- ⌘ Maintaining some type of continuity with the system's overall theme.

- ⌘ Matching the base medium and size so that randomness is maintained.

- ⌘ Ensuring that the new emblems fill in or augment those concepts you felt were missing originally (this means that you may go through this process more than once, should you discover other limitations in the present media).

- ⌘ Keeping any parts that you remove in a safe place. (You may want or need them sometime in the future.)

- ⌘ Recording the meaning of the new symbols, including any variance in meaning depending on where they come up in a reading.

The beauty of adaptation is that if you find the new symbol doesn't work out, you can just keep trying till you get it just right!

Making Your Own Divination System

Considering that people throughout history made their own divination systems, often out of whatever they had on hand, you're about to take part in a time-honored human tradition! Be forewarned, though, that this process can be a bit of an undertaking, filled with research and introspection. You cannot help but learn a lot about yourself and your perspectives in the process, however, which is always a good thing and well worth the time investment.

Steps for Making Your Own Divination System

1. Determine whether the system will be based on something that exists or something new.

2. Consider items in your sacred space of home as potential media.

3. Choose your base medium based on your life circumstances.

4. Decide on the size of the finished system (for example, number of symbols).

5. Decide if the system will be cast, scried, laid out, and so on.

6. Consider if the system can or will have upright and reversed meanings.

7. Decide on layout formats, if applicable, and what each space means.

8. Decide the interpretive value of your symbols alone and in combination with others.

9. Enact trial runs to work out the bugs and tweak the system to perfection.

10. Bless the system and start using it!

Let's look at this process step by step. First you're deciding whether to base your system on an existing concept or something wholly new. One person may wish to create his or her own tarot deck, while another may want to cast jelly beans. Neither method is "right" or "wrong" so long as both people approach their system respectfully.

In considering your base, bear in mind three things—what sense you respond most strongly, what kind of symbols appeal to you, and the complexity of your questions. The sensual cue will help you find a medium more easily (as mentioned before runes or stones are more tactile, for example). The symbols that appeal to you become important as the system develops. If you need more literal symbolism, you'll probably want a highly visual system, or one with emblems that are totally obvious to you when you see each. Finally, the complexity of your questions helps you figure out how many symbols you'll need.

Now look around your sacred space of home. As you will see in Part II, there are many items that can (and have) been used for divination that are handy and cost effective. These sample systems may spur an idea or two of your own. The advantage of this hearthside approach is that most of the items will already be saturated with your personal energy. They're also things with real meaning to your daily life. Both of these advantages equate to more accurate readings in the long haul.

Next comes your base media. You want to use something that's sturdy, for longevity, or at least find a way to protect more fragile systems. Hand colored cards, for example, should have a protective art spray coating to keep them from smudging. And while you might be thinking there aren't a lot of possibilities for media in your home, how about:

- Business cards.
- Colored pencils.
- Computer.
- Large buttons.
- Noodles.
- Nuts and bolts.
- Quotes.
- Ribbon.
- Shells.
- Sliced wood.
- Soap bubbles.
- Waxed leaves.

Many of these are reviewed in detail in Part II, so you might want to refer to that section for more ideas if you feel stumped.

As an aside, no matter what base you choose, I strongly advocate cleansing and blessing your system's components before you assemble them. (See "Care and Keeping of Your Tools" on page 65). The key is to begin with a system that's free of unwanted energies from the get-go so you can build a specific vibration that responds to you as you're making the set.

Once you have a base media, the next question is one of how many symbols. If you're only going to be asking yes or no questions, you don't need 70 emblems! However, most people have more detailed queries. My general suggestion is, minimally, to have 13 symbols in any set for diversity and to represent the major archetypes in human experience. Now, if you're really creative, even a binary tool (yes/no) can be adapted to include more potential symbolism. For example, if you've made an herb pendulum put thirteen items on the table around the area where you'll be observing it. Then if it swings toward a specific token, that clarifies your question more. (For more about using a pendulum with symbol sets, refer to pages 134-137 in Chapter 9).

NOTE: Each additional symbol in a system creates a new level of possible interpretations. The type of information you get from 21 runes versus the 64 symbols of the I Ching (some of which can actually transform into others) is dramatically different. Because you want to be happy with your final creation, consider these particulars seriously then decide how many emblems you want and *need*. Don't anticipate specifics from a highly generalized system.

Now you have the media and symbols in one spot. How will you use them? Will you lay them out like cards, draw them from a bag (like runes), or perhaps cast them over a surface (like crystals or maybe nuts and bolts)? Some divination systems will answer this question for you simply by their construct. In order to draw something from a bag, for example, each token must be the same size. Otherwise you can subconsciously learn which is which and skew the meaning of the reading. In effect, you're more likely to hear your hopes and fears than getting information from a more universal source. Conversely, an even-sized coupon set styled like a tarot deck can be laid out or drawn because you won't be able to tell one card from the other.

Whether or not your system is laid out, cast, or drawn, the next question to ask yourself is if you want reversed or negative meanings. These interpretive values imply obstacles or negative influences which must be overcome, something most situations have in common! There are some tarot readers who do not use reversed meanings at all. There are some people with cast systems that don't include a space on the casting surfaces for reversal meanings. However, it's my personal opinion that you're limiting the depth of information you could get by not having this option open. While not everything in life has a down side, when there is one, I personally like to have an inkling about it!

With all the information about your system in mind, you need to figure out what various placements of the elements in your system are going to indicate. It's easiest to explain this with several examples. With the pendulum I spoke of earlier, the yes or no answer was qualified by symbols placed around the dowsing area. If the pendulum swung toward one of those symbols, the meaning of that token altered the basic answer. For example, if the pendulum was swinging basically north/south (a yes) but toward a symbol that you designated as "caution," to me that means it's fine to move ahead, but slowly.

For any card set, you can use the basic layouts provided by various tarot decks as a starting point. A three-card layout, for example, might represent past issues, current energies, and future potentials (in that order) with regard to your question. A five-card spread might be Elemental. In this case, Earth would deal with mundane matters influencing your question; Air, communication issues; Fire, personal energy levels; Water, emotions; and Spirit, various energies. Note that this is an illustration provided to give you ideas. You can use it, adapt it, or make up layouts of your own. More examples of card layouts and reading can be found in Chapter 6 (see pages 100, 104, 112, and 113).

For cast systems you'll want to ponder whether the way they look (interpreting all parts as a whole, akin to an ink blot) or where they land determines the meaning. If the whole casting appears like a heart, I'd say that your emotions were a big part of the question, for example. On the other hand, if you want more details, where each part of the casting lands on a surface can give it more meaning. I have a set of stones that I use on a cloth with designations for the four Elements, four seasons, now/self and future/ impersonal. The center of my cloth is now and self (things that are taking place this moment or very personal to me). The edge of the cloth is the future possibilities or less personal influences. Any stone that lands off the cloth does not get read.

With each of these three examples I went back to a system similar to that which I was using for ideas. After all, some things have worked for hundreds of people over hundreds of years—there's no need to reinvent the wheel! What's most important at this juncture, however, is making note of what each symbol in your system means, and how placement affects that meaning. You're basically creating an interpretive book for yourself, a touchstone, to which you can return for continuity. A consistency of interpretation, except for those moments when Spirit guides your inner vision, helps make a system that regularly works together cohesively.

For recording your interpretive values, I suggest a spiral bound notebook as you may find the values of your symbols change during the trial period. Just trust me on this. Sometimes a divination system takes on a life all its own (which usually means you've done a great job with it). Better still, the time you take in delineating and defining your symbols, the easier you'll remember them and the more they absorb harmonic energy keyed to their value.

At last, its time to try the whole thing out. Get a couple of friends who don't mind being test subjects. After the reading, ask them what they thought was good or bad about the system. Was anything missing? Also do a self check to see if anything felt odd or different than you originally anticipated. Repeat this process several times until you have a reliable calibration on your system. From this point forward it's ready to be utilized.

Just one word of advice—leave yourself open to change. As with any system you may find even one you've made yourself needs revisions as your spirit grows and transforms. Let it grow with you!

Care and Keeping of Your Tools

As with any magickal tool, your divination system needs a little TLC. That TLC typically takes five forms, any of which can be further personalized by calling on a personal deity, using prayers from your faith, adding specially chosen incense, and so on.

Form one is blessing, which invokes divine favor not only for the divination system, but also for its user. Each reading opens a window into the collective unconscious. Your tool is about to become an instrument of universal energy, as are you. Consequently, a little spiritual guidance comes under the heading of "a good thing."

In looking at world religions, laying on of hands and praying is one way to direct blessings. Alternatively you might visualize, chant, or sing. What's most important is that you feel that special spark of sacred energies in your tool when you're done.

Form two is dedication. The purpose of a dedication is to commit, ordain, and consecrate your tool for its specific function in your life. If you're only reading this system for yourself, that specification should be part of your dedication. In this case you might add a few words such as, "I hereby dedicate this tool to my personal growth, awareness, and empowerment. May I always find truth herein." Don't worry about being flowery or fancy with your words, just make them meaningful to you. Say what's most important, keep your motives honed, and let your heart guide your words.

Form three is charging. Think of charging similarly to what you do with a battery that's run low. You bring more energy to it. To achieve this goal, each person has a slightly different form of "hookup" to the generator for power. One person places their tool in the light of the sun or moon (or both) to let it absorb conscious or intuitive energy respectively. The amount of time is really a personal matter. Some people use the symbolic value of numbers in making this decision (such as charging the tool for three hours in moonlight when their question has to do with relationships). Conversely a financial question might benefit more from four hours of sunlight (the number four is aligned with the Earth Element and temporal issues, and sunlight represents the rational mind).

A second type of charging uses visualization. For this, the practitioner holds his or her hands around the tool while envisioning pure, white light pouring into the item. This continues until he or she feels the system has been completely saturated with energy (some people say the tool becomes warm to the touch, which is how they know it's fully charged).

A third type of charging is Elementally based (and can also act as a cleansing). In this case, the practitioner puts their tool in water, soil, or sand or smudges it with smoke. Now, this approach is obviously limited by your media. If you have something that would be damaged by water, you will want to sprinkle water around it instead. Alternatively wrap the media to protect it from any harm, but so that it can still be surrounded by the Element you choose. By the way, you can key the charging Element to your question even as I illustrated with the use of sunlight and moonlight. For example, use soil when you've got an Earth-oriented question. This creates sympathy.

If you're not familiar with sympathetic magick, think of it like tuning a car radio. Using Elemental energies attunes your tool to the question at hand and provides better reception, consequently. And because charging or recharging can be done any time you feel the need, you can apply these ideas whenever you feel your system has picked up static or seems to be working oddly.

Finally, let me share a few ideas about storage and maintenance of your divination system. You'll want a safe place to keep the tool so that it doesn't randomly get handled or otherwise harmed. Some people just use a natural white fabric for this purpose; others have elaborate boxes and bundles. Really, anything that works and makes sense, considering the media, is fine.

Having a special housing for your tool has one nifty advantage: Each time you take the tool from its housing, you can mentally switch gears away from the temporal and toward the spiritual. With repeated use, this moment becomes a miniritual that puts you in the best possible frame of mind and spirit for the reading.

As far as maintenance goes, it's always a good idea to have some kind of routine cleansing and energizing for your system. The energy you've put into creating it won't last forever, and a tool can collect random vibrations when it's not in use, or from a reading if it's not purified afterward. So practice good spiritual hygiene when utilizing this system, even as you should for yourself.

Reading for Yourself, Others, and Groups

Now for the fun part—using your divination system. Right now you're in what I call the courtship stage of working with your divination tool(s). Be patient with yourself—it takes time to become proficient in any art. This isn't a fast food proposition where you can become a mystic overnight (with an order of fries on the side for when you get the munchies). This is about long-term satisfaction and success, not a quick fix. I promise the time you take in practice will *not* be wasted. It's an opportunity to sharpen your skills and think about spiritual symbols as they pertain to and affect your daily reality.

I share this with you because it ties into how one prepares for any reading, be it for yourself or others. You need to be mentally, physically, and spiritually attuned for what you're about to do. If you're overwrought, worried, distracted, sick, or find it difficult to separate personal feelings from the question at hand—it's not a good time to even try divination. No good will come from reading under any of those conditions. If anything, it's likely to be very confusing or negative.

Every practitioner has a personal way of knowing if they're in the right place to read, and many practitioners have little habits that help put them in a receptive state of mind. Most of these helpmates aren't even obvious. They include:

    ↝ Washing one's hands before touching the divination tools (symbolically a self-cleansing rite).

- Laying out a special surface on which the reading takes place (always doing so in a prescribed fashion).
- Stopping to breathe, focus, center, or pray.
- Meditating briefly with the querent, to establish a harmony of purpose.
- Anointing one's hands or third eye with an aromatic oil that elevates psychic energy.
- Invoking a guardian, guide, god, or goddess.
- Fasting a number of hours or days before the reading (a type of purification).

You can try any one of these or a combination, to see which ones work best for you, or create a preparation ritual all your own.

You're not the only element in a reading that needs to be prepared, however. There's also your working space. You want to create the right ambiance—one that's comfortable and inspires a spiritual state of mind. Just as you cleansed yourself, it doesn't hurt to smudge a reading space using cedar or sage before you begin. Again, you're just making sure to get rid of random energy that might hinder your accuracy. This is also a perfect time to make sure you won't get interrupted (turn off your cell phone). I personally like to light candles too. There's something about the soft light that helps me obtain spiritual awarenesses more easily.

If you're reading for yourself, I do issue some caution. Stick to things toward which you can maintain perspective. We're very close to our personal lives, and that makes objectivity very difficult in a reading. Divination tools can and will pick up your unspoken anxiety, wishes, hopes, and fears. As a result, the reading isn't really balanced or accurate. This is very natural and very human, so don't berate yourself if it happens. Rather, I suggest finding a reading partner with whom you can trade time. This way you have someone who's less emotionally involved, and therefore better able to provide the interpretation without additional "coloring."

When you're reading for others, there are also a few good guidelines to follow. They include:

- Making sure you're in the right frame of mind (if not, gently decline until another time).

- Making sure the person isn't just using you as a sideshow, or that they're not using divination as an ongoing crutch for decision making. Trust your instincts and the nudges of Spirit in making this determination.

- Making sure you have enough time for a good reading, with questions and clarifications afterward (this gives people closure).

- Making sure that privacy can be maintained.

- Making sure you have no negative feelings or personal opinions about the individual before you that could skew a reading (if so suggest someone else who might help them).

I have always consider reading to be a type of community service, but it takes a lot of energy and a certain amount of personal time, thus the guidelines. If you decide to go ahead with a reading, please give the person(s) before you the same type of input that you would want. In particular:

- Determine if you want to know the person's question or if you'd rather leave that open-ended for the review at the end of the reading.

- Remind the person that readings aren't infallible and what he or she does today with the information will affect their tomorrows.

∽ Endeavor to be a positive prophet (that is, share bad news in a positive, proactive way). No one should walk away from a reading feeling helpless or hopeless.

∽ Encourage the questioner to take notes or record the session. Many times the information received doesn't fully make sense until days or weeks later.

∽ Leave time at the end of the session for questions or clarification. This might mean having to draw more symbols out from your chosen media.

∽ Remain open to Spirit's small voice.

∽ Be honest. If the reading looks odd to you, tell the person that it doesn't seem to make sense, but continue to share what you see. I've had readings that seemed wholly "off" upon initial review but turned out to be completely meaningful to the questioner. On the other hand, I've also done readings for people where their lives were so filled with chaotic energy that no real answer was available at that time.

As you can imagine, things change a bit when you're not working just one-on-one. Group divination offers unique challenges. I've come up with several methods that seem to work in a group setting. I'll share both with you here, in case you'd like to try this sometime with a spiritual group that would like to improve rapport.

The first one uses stones: Everyone holds a small handful of tiny crystals (the smaller the better—I get mine so they're just larger than glitter) and thinks about a question, agreed upon ahead of time, that pertains to the whole group. After a few minutes, these get sprinkled on a surface covered with spray-on glue so they stick where they land. Everyone takes a turn sharing what he or she sees in the resulting patterns. Candles work similarly but each person chooses a color, holds the burning candle over the surface of the paper (no glue this time), and walks clockwise around the paper together letting the wax drip. The final patterns of wax are reviewed like one might look at an inkblot of many colors.

Another fun method of group divination begins by giving each person a slip of paper and pencil. Sit together, and have them visualize a huge bubble in the center of the room. Each person present puts a question into that bubble. Once the question is firmly in place, the group should breathe together for a few minutes then visualize the same bubble filling with radiant light. Scan that bubble for images, feelings or words, and write down whatever you receive. These missives can be put in a large bowl from which each person blindly pulls their answer to the question originally placed in the bubble.

The results from this activity are inevitably interesting. One person asks about whether he or she will travel soon and gets the word "boat" (which to my thinking says "yes"). Other person asks about his or her spiritual path and gets the word "owl" (this one is harder to interpret, but it could lead to exploring Athena or perhaps a Shamanic path in which owl is a messenger).

At the end of this activity, it's fun to put all the pieces of paper together and see if you can make sentences or if any of the pictures relate to each other. Discuss the possibilities as they relate to the group as a whole!

Hints for Success

- Be specific. Vague questions yield vague readings.

- Remember: Each divinatory system or technique determines how detailed your answer can be. Don't expect more from the diviner's kit than it can realistically give.

- Failure of a reading doesn't necessarily mean the system or reader is "bad." Each of us is still the master of our fate; keep in mind that you may be getting information you *need* instead of *want*, or perhaps the information simply isn't clear right now.

- When you get unclear results, try again another day and compare the two readings for clarification.

- How you internalize a reading is totally up to you—life is, indeed, what you make of it.

- Avoid using divination as a crutch, and avoid reading for people who seem to do likewise.

- Never peek at another's future without his or her permission. This is a breach of privacy akin to being a spiritual Peeping Tom.

- Always remain open to slight variations in interpretive values that may come from Spirit or a guide.

- Don't let divination be abused by experience-seekers or scoffers.

Last, but certainly not least, read with a loving heart and interpret with an open mind. Balance fact with faith. We cannot prove how or why divination works, we can only prove its results; I pray yours are always positive and life-affirming.

Part 2

Multipedia of Kitchen Divination Methods

Now for the fun part. You know how to find the best divination system for your personal use, how to adapt ready-made ones, and even what to think about when making your own kit. This part of the book helps you with that creation process by providing numerous examples of common household items that can be used as a system unto themselves, or as part of a larger media. Each method listed herein has instructions for its design (if needed) and, more importantly, example interpretive values for the results you may obtain when using that method.

For ease of reference, the chapters in this section are set up alphabetically, with Helpful Hints at the end. However, there are some instances where it made sense to lump several potential base media under one category. For example, the coupon tarot and greeting card tarot are listed in the chapter on *cards*. Similarly, potatoes, beans, and M&Ms are located in the *food findings* chapter, as each illustrates an edible media in which you can actually internalize the results of the readings by consuming them when you're done. (Yes, folks, for once it's not only okay to play with your food, it's encouraged!)

I encourage you just to review the headings before actually trying to make something. You're going to be pleasantly surprised at how many things in your home or on supermarket shelves have been and continue to be utilized as functional and enjoyable divinatory systems. When you're done looking them over, I also encourage you to walk through your living space to see what other ideas you come up with. Everything in and around your life has the potential to be utilized in a spiritual setting if you apply a little inventiveness and creativity. Once you begin seeing and applying that potential, it becomes natural, meaning your whole living environment will resonate with ongoing sacred energies.

What I'm providing is a step-by-step description of the creation process for illustration purposes only. This gives you a feel for how much work is involved in that particular tool, and what basic things you'll need to make each tool (such as paint, glue, and scissors). However, every tool that I'm describing here can be altered in a wide variety of ways to suit your fancy and inner vision. To encourage personalization, I have also given you a few examples of functional adaptations that hopefully inspire more ideas of your own.

Finally, following each system, you'll find some sample readings. These are provided to help you see how the whole tool works together, and what kind of results it can provide. As mentioned in Chapter 3, if you want highly detailed readings, you need a system with more symbols and potential combinations. Keep that in mind, when choosing which tools to make, so that your time and effort yields the most satisfying results.

Chapter 4

Boards

> *How can I tell the signals and signs by*
> *which one heart another heart divines?*
> —Henry Wadsworth Longfellow

Divination boards have a much longer history than you might expect. While most people recognize the Ouija, they might not know that this board may be related to a Hittite logographic divination system called *Kin*. The Kin was a board with two fields, each of which had symbols inscribed upon them. An object of some type was placed on or near the board and allowed to move of its own volition similarly to the pointer of the Ouija. Traditionally an elderly wise woman interpreted the results.

Another potential ancestor of the Ouija appeared in Greece around 371 C.E. It consisted of a wooden tripod (usually laurel), a round metal face with Greek lettering, and a ring suspended by linen thread. The ring was set in motion and observed. This particular method of fortune telling became so popular that it was used to determine the name of future emperors.

Beyond these two examples, the Romans, Chinese, Mongols, and even Native Americans had versions of board divination systems. Just 500 years ago, Native Americans used a painted board with special emblems called a *Squdilatc*. Rather than providing literal answers, the results were symbolic much like the boards I'll be describing shortly.

Because the Ouija has been turned into a game in our society, I typically do not recommend its use. It basically opens doors to any wandering spirit who might want to voice an opinion (not all of which are intended for the benefit of readers). Rather I'd like to offer three easy, homemade boards for your consideration. The first utilizes the top of a large metal canister, the second uses the bottom of a wooden wine box, and the third simply requires a flat surface.

Canister Top

The canister top divination board is actually based not only on the Ouija concept, but also a method called *tympania*. Vibrating surfaces such as drums or tambourines were utilized in Hungary, Siberia, and Lapland, usually in combination with beans, seeds, or shells. These media were placed in the middle of the vibrating surface, on which various emblems had been painted, and the surface tapped while the querente focuses on his or her question. Finally the results were interpreted.

To make one yourself, the first thing you need to do is obtain paint from a craft store that adheres to metal surfaces. (The acrylics used for metal fantasy figurines seem to work quite nicely.) You may wish to cover the entire inside of the top with one base color first, such as white, then paint your symbols over that base. This helps the images "pop" a bit from the background.

There's a lot of different ways you can set up the interior. One that I personally like is that of dividing the circle into 8 segments. Begin by marking the central point of your lid. If you wish, put a yin-yang emblem there, or something else personally meaningful. This location is from where your beans, seeds, or shells start out. Think of it like the central altar to this tool. The sacred markings bless, energize, and help guide the media.

Next, draw eight equidistant black lines from the center to the edge of the canister lid. This creates eight equal segments, looking much like a wheel. Now comes the fun part. What do you want to put in those segments? Because there are eight, you could use words and symbols for the four directions and the four seasons. Or, you might use images that represent the sabbats. You can also put several emblems into each section that represent various aspects of one theme. For example, if one of the eight sections symbolizes spring, you could have one symbol each for a new start, growth, and fertility (all of which are related to spring's energy).

Continuing with the seasons/Elements example for the basic design, I suggest the central area have the image of a flame to represent Spirit binding the Elements together. Next, set up the canister top with the Elements in their respective sections (namely North as Earth, East as Air, South as Fire, and West as Water). Using their associated colors of green, yellow, red, and blue (respectively), paint the entire portion with the Element's hue. The basic interpretive values for the Elements follow:

- **Earth:** Monetary issues, personal growth, physical health.
- **Air:** Communication, understanding, motivation.
- **Fire:** Energy levels, passions, perspectives (vision).
- **Water:** Emotions, intuition, spirituality.

Next, paint the four seasons in the northeast, southeast, southwest, and northwest areas, with three emblems each inside as follows (each symbol's basic meaning follows in parentheses):

- **Spring:** Northeast; a rising sun (beginnings), a seed (fertility), a sprout (growth).
- **Summer:** Southeast; a full sun (energy), a stick person (socialization), a flower or berry (abundance and fruition).
- **Fall:** Southwest; a leaf (cycles and change), a pumpkin (protection), a cornucopia (bounty).
- **Winter:** Northwest; a snowflake (slowing down), a bare tree (rest), a package (gifts or messages).

Let this dry completely and then spray the surface with a clear protective art spray. This helps keep the paint from chipping in the future.

Now to use the system! Get three white beans and three black beans. The white beans are positive indicators, the black ones negative. Put those in the middle of the board. Next you can either hold the canister top in one hand and tap the underside with your other, or put it on a flat surface and tap the edge with a chopstick or butter knife. Close your eyes while you tap, focusing on your question. Stop whenever you feel you should (when you feel as if your question has been directed fully to the media). Now look at where the beans landed and interpret the results.

Sample Reading

The question: Let's say your question was about a relationship.

The reading: One white bean landed in Fire, while a black one landed on the full summer sun (the remaining beans stayed in the center). To me this indicates a problem. Either your relationship has a lot of infighting or it's too passionate (meaning it's likely to burn out).

The question: Another example pertains to a job-oriented question.

The reading: Say a white bean landed on spring's rising sun, another white bean landed on Earth, and a black one landed on the leaf. This is still a very good reading. It implies you have the potential of a good job that will provide for your needs, but it requires making some changes to achieve your goal.

Symbol Board

Some folks like using a symbol board more so than the canister top because the wooden media seems more natural. Also, depending on the type of wine box you use, you may be able to store the parts to this system neatly inside!

NOTE: If you can't find a wine box, you may be able to locate a wooden crate with a solid bottom at a second hand store. I advise looking for something that's about 14 inches × 12 inches so that it's fairly portable and can rest easily in your lap.

As with the canister top, step one is determining how many sections your board should have. You can either divide up the interior in a way so that each section is the same size, or you could make the configuration a little more random. For the first option, you'll want your spaces to each be about 2 inches square, to afford enough room for clear interior symbols. The larger your separators, the fewer symbols you can utilize.

Measure out the sections, marking with a pencil, then paint in borderlines following the pencil marks. Black is a good color for this as it stands out clearly. However, some people use silver-toned divisions because (to them) it symbolizes intuitive, lunar nature.

Next you need to choose 42 symbols to go into the squares. These symbols can be painted into each space, or (because you're working with wood) decoupage is kind of fun. This process also provides you with lots of color and image options that you might not have if your painting skills (like mine) are lacking.

──────DECOUPAGE BASICS FOR BEGINNERS──────

Supplies:

- Decorative paper cutouts.
- Scissors or X-acto knife.
- Glue (Elmer's or something similar is fine).
- Paintbrushes (for applying paint, glue, and varnish).
- Acrylic varnish.

The word *decoupage* comes from a French term meaning "to cut up." This method was used in Europe a lot during the 17th and 18th centuries. It also became very popular in Victorian America.

You can use nearly any type of paper image for decoupage, including greeting cards, wallpaper, magazine images, wrapping paper, and so on. Note, however, that the inside of your box needs to be clean and dust free. If it's rough, it will need to be sanded so the images and varnish finish flat and last longer. If you want the bottom of the box to have a coat of paint, you'll need to do that after sanding and let it dry for 24 hours. Be sure to work on a protected surface (lay down newspapers or a plastic bag).

When cutting out your images, watch the space you've got. Your edges should be smooth. Lay these out in the box, trying various configurations until you're happy with the diversity and overall visual impact of the symbols.

Use a paintbrush to apply the glue to the back of the picture, then put that image in the space you've chosen. Continue this way until all your images are in place. You can put more than one image in a square to create layering and more interpretive values. (If you find you have air bubbles or bumps, a small paint roller applied gently over the top of the image, while the glue is still wet, should fix the problem.) Let the glue dry completely.

Finally apply a light coat of varnish. I recommend that you use at least 10 coats, but each coat must dry completely before adding the next. This is a bit time-consuming, but protects your finished board from wear and tear.

What type of symbols might you use for the decoupage box? Well, you could consider a theme. For example, if you love to garden how about images of specific flowers, plants, and herbs that you recognize? The symbolic value of each, in this case, could be based on the lore of the plant. If you love to cook, you could have images of various fruits, vegetables, and beverages, again basing the interpretations on the metaphysical association for each item. Because I'm a Kitchen Witch, I'll use this second theme as an illustration. Following are some sample symbols and their meanings for the culinary-themed divination box:

- **Alfalfa sprouts:** Providence, abundance.
- **Apple:** Health, peace, love.
- **Bay leaf:** Psychic powers, strength.
- **Blender:** Mingling energies into a harmonious whole.
- **Bread:** Kinship, sustenance.
- **Cake:** Celebration, hospitality, joy.
- **Chicken:** Recuperation, well-being.
- **Egg:** Fertility, unanswerable questions.
- **Food wrap:** Conservation, frugality.
- **Grapes:** Dreams and visions.
- **Milk:** Goddess energy, maternal instinct, nurturing.
- **Oven:** Fire Element, womb symbol, slow transformation.
- **Pear:** Longevity and luck.
- **Strawberry:** Zeal, romance.

· **Thermometer:** Gauging situations, careful observation.

· **Whisk:** Excitement.

· **Wine:** Relaxation, hospitality, joyous occasions.

While I haven't given you 42 here, I think you can see where I'm going. I should also note that your box doesn't have to have any particular theme. You could mix hand-painted runes with various decoupage imagery that appeals to you and have it work just fine.

The second form of the symbol box using a random configuration works similarly, but for the fact that the symbols aren't laid out in such a distinct, even pattern. One person might choose to paint the Tree of Life, for example, and utilize the meanings behind the 10 points thereon. Another person might paint runes spread out in a circle and use their traditional meanings. As you can see this is a highly adaptable system with lots of options from which to choose.

The two important thing are that you choose a combination that offers a wide variety of interpretive value and that the images are immediately meaningful to you.

Once the box is completed, there are two different ways to use it. You can toss colored beans on the surface, similar to how the canister top was used (dark ones being a negative or reversed value), or you can toss dice onto the surface and add in the symbolic value of the number showing on each. Both approaches work very well, but working with a nonperishable such as dice is nice (that way you can keep the set together).

SAMPLE READING

The question: A new relationship has taken a more serious turn, and the question regards its future potential.

The reading: This reading utilizes the bean method. One white bean landed on the strawberry, and one on the bread, while one black one landed on the whisk. The interpretation here is that the relationship has strong potential but you need to tone down your level of enthusiasm so you don't burn out (or worse, scare the person off).

The question: You inquire about moving to another part of the country without a job prospect.

The reading: This reading utilizes two dice. The number 1 landed on the thermometer, while the number 4 landed on the oven. It's interesting here that both symbols imply "heat" (as in taking some heat!). Overall the reading is very cautious, implying that more thought and planning are highly recommended. This proverbial loaf isn't fully cooked yet—put it on the back burner until you've had more time to get a sound plan in order. (For more on numerical associations, see pages 120-122.)

Fortune Tablets

Fortune tablets were popularized by the Egyptian Magi. Rather than symbols, the fortune boards use numbers, each of which has a corresponding interpretation. Some of these tablets were incredibly detailed. Cornelius Agrippa, a mystic/alchemist of the early 1500s, had a lengthy set of questions on which he would ask the querent to focus, and he limited the times during which he used the tablet to only auspicious days.

To make your own tablet, you can use any flat surface (even paper, but it's likely you'll want to make one that's more permanent.) The shape and arrangement pertain to the nature of the matters addressed. For more Earthly matters, pattern the numbers 1 through 25 in a square or rectangle as shown here (squares represent the Earth Element):

25	6	8	22	2	11
15	13	17	3	24	
5	7	1	12	4	
14	18	9	23	20	
	16		10	19	21

Leave enough space between each number so that you can determine clearly which one you've landed on when using a pencil or other type of pointer (I use a chop stick).

Now, close your eyes and consider a question (in the case of Earth matters, specifically one centered on finances, work, the rational mind, your physical nature, growth, cycles, and so forth). Continuing to focus on that question, let your hand with the pointer fall to the surface of the board. Read the number that's closest to the point. The basic interpretations follow:

· **1:** Improvements with business and better foundations.

· **2:** Legal problems or failures (check the fine print).

· **3:** A major change, often preceded by news.

· **4:** Financial setback.

· **5:** Unknown information or secrets that need to be revealed before making a decision or move.

· **6:** Lots of red tape; getting nowhere fast.

· **7:** A good partnership can help you.

· **8:** A sense of personal or group fulfillment.

· **9:** Sudden opportunity; look at it cautiously and carefully.

· **10:** Travel and adventure on the horizon.

· **11:** You have a good reason to be wary.

· **12:** Victory or a successful outcome (specifically from your efforts).

· **13:** Avoid borrowing money or asking for favors.

· **14:** A new project or possibly a baby.

· **15:** The respect of friends; honor.

· **16:** New people will help you; look at this situation in a new way.

· **17:** Loss of status; dishonor.

· **18:** Advantageous developments (often with a person or group).

· **19:** Misuse of someone's charitable nature.

· **20:** Irresponsibility; procrastination causes trouble.

· **21:** News about your health.

· **22:** Listen to both your heart and your head in this.

· **23:** Hidden or unknown matters; either wait or proceed very slowly.

· **24:** Think before you speak or act.

· **25:** Personal character flaws may bite you.

· **Blank area:** No answer available.

If you'd like to make a tablet focused on more intuitive and spiritual information, use a circle with the numbers 1–13 randomly placed around the edge (13 is a lunar number and corresponds with the psychic self). Just as before, focus on a question that pertains to things such as your spiritual path, your gut instincts, inspiration, creativity, fertility, dreams, and travel. Let your hand with the pointer drop once again. Basic interpretive values are as follows:

· **1:** Patience and practice are the keys to success.

· **2:** If walls could talk, what would this one be saying?

· **3:** Stop worrying about others, listen to your inner voice.

· **4:** Learn how to give to yourself and how to receive from others.

· **5:** You're out of balance; regroup.

· **6:** Put the foundations under your hopes and dreams (in other words, stop wishing and start doing).

· **7:** The answers or inspiration you seek will come from an acquaintance.

· **8:** Use rationality and logic to answer this question.

· **9:** Be aware that answers often come in a way you *need* instead of what you *want*.

· **10:** Bad timing.

· **11:** Seek out the truth and make sure you get all of it.

· **12:** Stand up for what you want or what you
believe and success follows.

· **13:** Fulfillment; success.

· **Blank area:** No answer available.

Notice that both of these tablets can easily be expanded.
In terms of interpretive values, your expansions might be
based on numerology or on what a number means to your
personally. If you expand either system, you can actually
drop your pointer hand more than once to get improved
details.

SAMPLE READING

The question: Say you are looking for a coven and ask
about whether or not you should consider join-
ing a new coven forming in your area.

The reading: Using the round tablet as an example,
let's say the first number your pointer falls upon
is 2, followed by 10. From these two numbers, my
best guess is that there's a very good reason you
have not, as yet, found a coven and this one
doesn't seem quite right either. Being with the
right group is well worth waiting for, so it seems
the tablet advises patience.

Chapter 5

Candles

*The best way to predict the future is to
invent it.*

—Alan Kay

Divination employing candles is a subclass of *pyromancy* (divination by fire). If one observes the candle itself for signs (the behavior of the wax while still part of the candle), that's formally called *lychnomancy*. Watching the flame is *pyroscopy*, while observing wax drippings is *ceromancy*. Confused yet? Don't feel bad, you're not alone. Historians also often found themselves trying to discern exactly what was what, especially when you begin to add in things like *lapandomancy* (torch observation), and Egyptian and Tibetan wick interpretations (the former of which I never found a name for, and the latter of which was called *mapo).*

If you love candles and want to use them for divination, you have plenty of company among our ancestors. Even Nostradamus used these little bundles of wax to inspire his writings, one quote from which reads "Secrets are revealed by the subtle spirits of fire." Because our ancestors had candles around all the time for light, it's not surprising to learn they utilized them as a divinatory system too. In fact, there are few cultures that I could find that didn't utilize at least one part of a candle for fortune telling! For example, the Irish chose a specially colored candle (the color symbolized the nature of the question) and then burned it at midnight during a waxing or full moon. The observations of the candle and wax created the interpretive values.

I'll be sharing with you several methods that employ candles as a media shortly, but first let's consider making our own specially charged candles for this purpose. Anyone who has ever attended summer camp has probably made the infamous milk carton candle. Any similar waxed container (like that for heavy creamer or orange juice) will also work quite well if you'd prefer something smaller. Alternatively use a metal cooking form that you've oiled thoroughly (however, if you scent the candle wax, you may not want to use this container again for culinary purposes, as some candle scents contain substances that should not be ingested). Inexpensive metal containers can often be obtained for as little as a dollar or less at second hand stores if you'd rather not use your daily cookware.

For more information on candle making, check out:

- *http://members.iinet.net.au/~campbell1/candles.htm*.
- *http://www.candletech.com/*.
- *http://www.luminacandles.com/instruct.htm*.
- *Exploring Candle Magick* by New Page Books.

If you feel like getting really fancy, swing by a hobby and craft supply store for a mold that somehow represents the candle's purpose. I've seen wonderful five-pointed star molds that are ideal for symbolizing the balance of energies in the pentagram, for example. This is also a great place to buy wax if you don't have a bundle of candle ends and pieces at home ready to remelt.

Once you've chosen a container, step two is melting the wax. Now, bear in mind that this step includes adding color, aromatics, and other symbolic elements, so you need to think ahead. White is a perfectly acceptable color for all magickal candles (it's neutral), however you may wish to use a color that better symbolizes the candle's function (yellow for divination) or your question (like red for love and passion, green for money, purple for spiritual questions, and so on). Aromatics work similarly. I recommend using oils, as opposed to finely ground herbs, for safety reasons. Herbs can spark when you burn the candle if not properly integrated.

When heating the wax, use a medium-low setting so it melts evenly and so it won't catch fire or cause a serious burn if accidentally spilled. While you're melting the wax, it's a perfect time to prepare your container. If you're using a milk carton, the inside is already smooth with wax. Other containers, however, should be oiled lightly (I use a cooking spray—it's fast and easy). This is also a good moment to bless your wax with an incantation, visualization, or prayer that empowers its function in your magick. Here's a sample prayer:

> Sacred Parent, Power of All Creation,
> see this simple tool, and bless it for my arts.
> When the light of this candle shines,
> let my inner sight see clearly,
> through the clouds of uncertainty.
> As the flame burns, let truth come
> to my mind and heart.
> So mote it be.

Let the wax cool a bit before pouring it into your mold. I like to stir mine so the temperature is even throughout.

Once poured, you'll have to let it cool at room temperature for several hours (remember the center of the candle takes longer to cool than the edges). Usually I just leave it overnight, to be on the safe side. Remember to be careful cleaning up, so no melted wax goes down the sink, where it will harden and clog the drain.

To release your candle from it's housing, simply dip it in hot water momentarily. Take care not to submerge the top of the mold, as you do not want to get the wick wet. Turn the candle out upside down onto a wax paper surface (you can repeat the dipping two or three times until it simply slides out). At this juncture your candle is ready for placing into a suitable holder or to be carved with symbols or imagery that, again, supports your goal. By the way, if you won't be using your candle immediately or plan to store it between uses, I recommend wrapping it with a linen cloth and putting it in a plastic bag. Label the bag with the theme for which you've created the candle (general divination, love, luck, and so on). That way you'll be able to use the energies you've placed therein more effectively in the future, should you forget which candle is which!

Now that your candle is ready to use, we'll explore two types of candle divination—observing the movements and behavior of the candle's flame and observing drippings of the candle's melted wax.

Candle Flame Observations

Light your candle with your question in mind. The act of lighting your candle is a function of will—your focus here is important. Close your eyes for a moment and conceptualize your question with as much depth and dimension as possible. Now open your eyes and watch the flame's movement. Interpretations are as follows:

· **Bright, dancing flame:** A very positive answer. Also an indication of good health.

· **Pale flames:** Illness or negative changes on the horizon (also indicates bad weather—figuratively or literally).

· **Sudden blazing:** Troubles; a stranger with a message; an angry flare-up.

· **Blue flames:** A spirit's presence; storms on the horizon.

· **Candle refuses to light:** A very negative omen; difficulties await.

· **Sparks:** Anger or passions revealed; forthcoming news.

· **Crackling:** A frosty emotional state.

· **Smoldering:** Bitterness and troubles.

· **Small or dim flame:** Hold off on any decisions; timing is bad.

· **Flame splits:** More than one option available; feeling divided.

· **Fire burns candle on left side:** Bad news for love (note this can be anything you love, a job, an art, a person, and so forth).

· **Average flame, lots of movement:** Change.

SAMPLE READING

The question: Let's say your home has been filled with tension and you were considering a family meeting to resolve it. You ask the candle if the time is right.

The reading: If the resulting flame remains small, your answer is "not now." If the candle flares up or sparks, then burns with a large flame, the answer is yes, but be prepared for some arguing. If the candle smokes or crackles, people's emotions are probably too highly charged right now for any productive result.

Wax on Water or Paper

Scrying the patterns created by wax when it drips into water or onto a paper surface was a system used by Romans, the Spanish, Mexicans, and Haitians, just to name a few. Frequently the color of the candle was chosen to represent the question's theme. Alternatively, the candle might be dressed (dabbed with aromatic oil from the center outward), the scent likewise mirroring the question. I personally like to combine these and use two candles (one white and one based on my question). I've found that having more than one color improves my personal ability to discern shapes, and it may help you too if you find you experience problems.

Again, focus and have your question in mind as you light the candle. If you are using paper, be sure it is an appropriate size (especially if you're doing a group reading, you want a large enough piece of paper so that your

companions can circle around it comfortably) and thick enough that the wax won't bleed through. Practically any container will work for dripping onto water. To interpret your wax drippings first look at the whole pattern created to see if anything pops out at you. Then examine any small parts that seem to have a recognizable shape. Don't look too hard, in fact unfocusing your eyes a bit helps. These aren't going to be perfect geometric images—they're semblances of images that touch our subconscious and superconscious mind.

SAMPLE READING

The question: You pose a question regarding a serious relationship.

The reading: If you see, for example, a heart pattern that slowly divides, it talks of a relationship or partnership in trouble to the point of potential separation. If the heart is close to the center of the surface, the situation is present and very personal. If it's closer to the edge of the surface, it's more distant in time or deals with an acquaintance. As for what other images mean, I suggest referring to any resource for tea leaf patterns or ink blots, as this system works similarly (I provide a brief list of interpretive values in tea leaf reading on page 169-172).

Chapter 6

Cards

> *The measure of our future success and happiness will not be the quality of the cards we are dealt by unseen hands, but the poise and wisdom with which we play them.*
>
> *Choose to play each hand to the best of your ability without wasting the time or energy it takes to complain about either the cards or the dealer or the often unfair rules of the game.*
>
> *Play both the winning and the losing hands as best you can, then fold the cards and ante up for the next deal!*
>
> —Joe Klock

Various systems of divining with cards have existed around the globe, the most commonly known being the tarot, which is first mentioned in a Swiss manuscript circa 1377. By the 16th century, cartomancy was becoming very popular and was even reportedly enacted for Mary, Queen of Scots. Sadly that reading came up all spades, and preceded her arrest and execution. On a slightly less grim note, Marie Le Normand was a professional cartomancer in Paris, starting in 1790, with a rather notable list of clients—including Napoleon!

The nice part about card systems is that homemade versions may be easily created from pretty basic materials. In fact, you can even use a standard deck of playing cards, if you have one handy.

Using a Regular Deck of Cards

When using a regular deck of cards, you can approach the reading in one of two ways. First, you could look at the symbols as having equivalent values to that of a tarot deck without the Higher Arcana. The absence of these cards won't really hinder your reading but that you won't be seeing those archetypal images and energies in relation to the rest of your layout. If you choose this approach, the suit of Cups becomes Hearts, Coins becomes Diamonds, Swords becomes Spades, and the suit of Rods becomes Clubs. The Jacks equate to the "Pages" of each suit. And, of course, you can use all the same types of layouts as you do with tarot decks.

Now, if you'd like to try something a little different, interpret a layout according to the following values, which seem to have been popular in Spain around the same time that Ms. Normand was enjoying success elsewhere. You begin by holding the deck in your hands and thinking of a question. Shuffle the cards while continuing to focus on that question. Use any type of layout you wish (such as three cards for *past/present/future*, five cards for *situation/ underlying energies/action called for/obstacles/outcome*, and so on). Put down however many cards the layout calls for, either pulling them randomly from the deck or directly from the top (trust your instincts). Look up the meanings on this list:

♣ Clubs ♣

- **Ace:** Joy and abundance.
- **King:** A person who is forthright, kind, and a good leader.
- **Queen:** A romantic person with charitable tendencies.
- **Jack:** A bright, energetic young person who is very giving.
- **10:** Improvements, especially in finances.
- **9:** Unexpected gift or gains.
- **8:** Attention and affection from someone helps your situation.
- **7:** Recovery or turnaround.
- **6:** Success or prosperity.
- **5:** Social occasions or unexpected news.
- **4:** A setback or disappointment.
- **3:** Anger, but not without resolution.
- **2:** Frugality is called for; be careful.

♥ Hearts ♥

- **Ace:** Good news, especially for a relationship or partnership.
- **King:** A liberal person.
- **Queen:** A gentle, kind person with great beauty.
- **Jack:** A young person fond of risk and adventure.
- **10:** Overcoming the odds.
- **9:** A personal hope fulfilled.
- **8:** Affection returned.
- **7:** Good relationships; peace with self.
- **6:** Unexpected turn for the better.
- **5:** Heed advice from a respected person.

· **4:** Change in residence or work.

· **3:** Troubles ahead.

· **2:** New friends or partners.

♦ Diamonds ♦

· **Ace:** A sports-like outing or time in nature.

· **King:** A temperamental, shrewd, and dangerous
person.

· **Queen:** A gossip monger.

· **Jack:** A deceptive, unfaithful younger person.

· **10:** Movement or change.

· **9:** Delays and nuisances (red tape).

· **8:** Passion and romance.

· **7:** Take some time for yourself; get perspective.

· **6:** Healing or reconciliation.

· **5:** Business improvements.

· **4:** Slow, steady progress.

· **3:** Legal difficulties, especially in a relationship.

· **2:** New or refreshed love (including self love).

♠ Spades ♠

· **Ace:** General pleasures and pleasantries.

· **King:** An envious person who causes problems.

· **Queen:** A single person who has your best interest
in mind.

· **Jack:** Someone plotting mischief.

· **10:** Bad news and sadness.

· **9:** Death (literal or figurative).

· **8:** Bad luck; plans undone; watch your health.

· **7:** Minor troubles and misunderstandings.

· **6:** Reversal.

· **5:** Let your friends help you.

· **4:** Struggles in business or love.

· **3:** Sadness and separation.

· **2:** Fraud or treachery.

NOTE: Some readers don't used reversed meanings. (In fact, the faces of some cards look the same upside-down!) If you want to include reversed meanings in your readings, use indelible ink to mark either the "top" or "bottom." When the cards come up reversed, you can likewise reverse their meanings. For example, if the two of spades comes up reversed, that could mean that what you perceive as a lie isn't, or that perhaps someone doesn't know the whole truth but they're not being purposefully deceptive.

Also, face cards coming up in groupings of two, three, or four have specific importance as follows:

· **Four Aces:** Danger of failure; be wary.

· **Three Aces:** Very good news.

· **Two Aces:** A plot is laid against you.

· **Four Kings:** Honor and reward comes from hard work.

· **Three Kings:** Important advice or business dealings.

· **Two Kings:** Partnership (a good one).

· **Four Queens:** Social gathering of some importance.

· **Three Queens:** Watch for an unusual phone call.

· **Two Queens:** See that friend you've been thinking about.

· **Four Jacks:** A group of young people; having fun.

· **Three Jacks:** Untrue friend or purposeful deceit.

· **Two Jacks:** Malice and hidden agendas.

SAMPLE READING

The question: Let's say a person is wondering about the overall energies influencing their lives at this moment.

The reading: Utilizing a four-card spread (for Earth, Air, Fire, and Water), the cards that come up are the King of Clubs, 5 of Hearts, 7 of Spades, and 4 of Spades. Because the Earth position deals with matters of business or money, the King of Clubs implies that a kindly person can help you if you're in a bit of financial trouble. In the Air position, the 5 of Hearts supports the first card by instructing the querent to really *listen* to this person's advice. Meanwhile, however, the 7 of Spades implies that some of the querent's problems stem from an argument or miscommunication. This card is further supported by the Water card, which says that problem was with a coworker or loved one. So, while it seems there is a solution to the present turmoil, it will require mending fences and cleaning out surrounding residual negativity.

Greeting Cards

If tarot cards or regular playing cards don't appeal to you, how about creating your own system out of greeting cards that you save throughout the year. Think about it. Friends and family alike looked for a special card to say something to you in a unique way. That message and that energy of good intention remains in the greeting cards, thereby providing you with an extra boost to enable more accurate readings!

To make this system, you'll want to keep the covers from cards that are of the same size and shape (this is important in order to keep the system random). Once you have a goodly number (I recommend at least 13), you can laminate them or treat them with some art spray for longevity. You could also cut out the central images and put them on blank cards in a decoupage style (see the instructions for decoupage on pages 82-83). Note that if you choose this approach it won't matter what size the original greeting cards were, only that the *finished* cards are all of matching size.

The next step is that of assigning value to each card. Because most cards had a defined purpose it shouldn't be too difficult to come up with interpretations. For example, a card with a couple on the front that says "Love" would be a logical choice to which to assign the interpretive value of relationships (specifically intimate ones). Similarly, cards showing a handsome man, a younger child, or a beautiful woman might correlate to any of the four Knight or King cards, the Page cards, and the Queen cards in the tarot.

Now, if you have a blank card with scenery, or you're just using the image on a card and no words, you have a little more "wiggle room" with the meaning. To illustrate, a friend sent me a card with kittens playing on the cover (no words). The meaning I assigned to this card upright is "Get out and play with your friends—you're taking things too seriously. Reconnect with the inner child and let her out!" The reversed meaning is "There's a time and place for everything, and now is not the time for distraction. Turn your attention back to more serious matters and leave the playing for later."

Another good illustration is a party-oriented card with balloons on it. In this case, you could cut out the balloons, put them on a precut card surface and interpret something (upright) such as "A reason for celebration or a positive turn of events. Your burdens should be easing, and your emotions lifting." The reversed interpretation might be "A hope or wish gone awry. It may have been proverbially 'full of hot air' or simply mistimed. Go back to square one and rethink your strategy."

Now if the image on the original card is more complex or abstract, the interpretive value you can give it can also be more complex (if you wish) or less literal. The more details you have, the closer you come to allowing for interpretations akin to what a tarot deck provides.

Step three (after recording your card's values) is determining what type of layouts you want to use. Really, any layout that you've used in tarot will work with the greeting card deck, so long as there aren't more spaces in the layout than you have cards. Last but not least, give it a trial run using two or three layouts. Make notes of your experience.

Because of the vast diversity of potential symbols you could assemble in this deck, I'm not providing a sample reading here.

Coupons

Think for a moment about how much money the marketing department of a company pays to determine the name of a product, and how much more they pay for specially designed advertisements. The whole goal is to get the consumer's attention (namely you and me). The advertiser and marketer manage this feat by trying to appeal to your senses, emotions, and the subconscious mind. Therefore, all the key elements are in place to make a coupon "tarot" quite functional.

Symbolically, I don't recommend using "expired" coupons. To my thinking that means their "power" has been drained completely. On the other hand, it might be a nice way to recycle. Think about how you feel about this, and make your choice accordingly.

Collecting coupons isn't hard. Typically a huge bundle arrives at my house every few weeks, not to mention those that come in magazines and newspapers. In terms of what to collect—look at the product's name or the overall imagery of the coupon even as you did with the greeting cards. Next, mount the coupons on blank pieces of sturdy poster board (of the same size and shape). This way you can use nearly any coupon you happen across without worrying about comparative sizes. I also recommend covering the cards with lamination or art spray for longevity. Here's a small sampling of some with possible interpretive values:

Product	*Upright Meaning*	*Reversed Meaning*
Air freshener	A chance to clear the air and your name.	Something stinks about this situation.
Bandages	Slow, steady healing (emotional, physical, or spiritual).	Caution; safety first!
Book club	Matters of learning and logic.	Not paying enough attention to the rational self.
Bread	Providence. You will have what you need.	The need for frugality.
Candles	The hidden will be revealed.	You're totally in the dark on this one. Don't proceed until you know more.
Chicken soup	Recovery and improved health.	Take care not to overextend personal energies; watch your health.
Coffee	A boost in personal energy.	Loss of interest or zeal (feeling weary).
Film	Live in the moment; seize the day!	Check your perspectives; something's amiss.
Joy (detergent)	Happiness, success.	Setbacks or saddness.
Mouthwash	Pleasant discourse.	Watch the way you communicate (your intention is not being understood.
Pain reliever	Resolution and reduction of stress.	Situations that cause you literal or figurative headaches.

NOTE: Some of these examples could be further de-
lineated. For example, the flavor of the mouthwash
could provide extra symbolism, as could the aroma
of the air freshener.

SAMPLE READING

The question: The question posed had to do with problems in a friendship.

The reading: The three coupon-cards (for past,
present, and future) pulled were Book Club (upright), Film (reversed), and Bandages (upright).
This implies that you and your friend initially
connected on a strong mental level (perhaps meeting in school). However, right now you're not
seeing things accurately. Take a few steps back
and try seeing things from your friend's perspective. If you do, the outcome card implies that the
relationship will heal, slowly and steadily.

Monopoly

As the parent of three children I have more than my
fair share of games with missing parts—Trivial Pursuit
and Monopoly being but two. That situation lead me to
ponder the option of using the leftover parts in divination.
Let's use Monopoly as an example, because it actually
offers two different possibilities. The first would be a
cast system (see Chapter 7 on page 115) utilizing the
player pieces, each one of which would have a different
meaning depending on where it landed on your casting
surface. In fact, you might be able to combine these tokens
with one of the board systems mentioned in Chapter 4,
to increase interpretive details.

As for the Monopoly cards, the beauty of using them is that there's no work involved other than determining your interpretive values (unless you prefer to trim the cards all to a similar size, to promote randomness). Following are some example interpretations:

Card	*Upright Meaning*	*Reversed Meaning*
Go to Jail	Legal matters and red tape stall plans.	A victory in court or a settlement.
Pass "Go," collect $200	An unexpected gift or bonus (especially if this appears with Park Place).	The money you need is slow in coming; be frugal.
Railroad	Travel or adventure on the horizon.	Plans to go abroad derailed, often by technical troubles.
Pay tax	Unanticipated expenditures, often due to something you've overlooked.	Small financial relief when you need it most.

Continue writing up whatever cards you've chosen to include in your system and give it a try! Just one word of caution: Because cards such as these have been used as a toy up to this point, you may wish to cleanse and bless those you're going to use for divination. That helps negate any residuals from their previous incarnation!

Flower Power

Divination utilizing flowers comes under both the formal titles of *botanomancy* and *florimancy*, the second pertaining only to flowers while the first designation covers any plant matter. Hawaiians and ancient Greeks both had floral systems of divination. This one, however, is based on the Victorian language of flowers.

Let me backtrack for a moment. During the Victorian era young lovers were precluded from being overtly open about their feelings (it simply was a social faux pax!). So, when a book called *Language of Flowers*, by Miss Corruthers of Iverness, appeared in 1879, people cleverly used nature's words to convey what society would not allow. This symbolic language is still often used in the floral industry to this day! Here's a brief list of common plants included in this language and their meanings:

- **Basil:** Hatred or ire.
- **Bay leaf:** Transformation.
- **Buttercup:** Wealth and wishes.
- **Carnation:** Honor or esteem.
- **Daisy:** Innocence and naïveté.
- **Dandelion:** Omens, signs (messages).
- **Evergreen:** Worthiness.
- **Foxglove:** Ambition (effort).
- **Geranium:** Memory.
- **Hawthorn:** Hope renewed.
- **Heather:** Hermitage.
- **Holly:** Foreknowledge.
- **Honeysuckle:** Devotion.
- **Iris:** News.
- **Ivy:** Companionship.
- **Jasmine:** Friends.
- **Lavender:** Answers.
- **Lilac:** New love.
- **Lily:** Happiness.
- **Marigold:** Sadness.
- **Mistletoe:** Victory.
- **Primrose:** Tenacity.
- **Rose:** Beauty and love.

· **Sweet William:** Deception.

· **Thyme:** Bravery.

· **Violet:** Devotion.

The floral system I'm suggesting here utilizes the decoupage technique we've already discussed (see page 82). As an aside, it is also representative of the very first divination system I made for myself because I love working with plants and herbs. To begin, you'll either need to gather pictures of specific flowers or plants, or harvest, press, and dry living plants that you wish to use. The second method is lovely, as it speaks directly with the language and energy of nature (however, the first method is a little more Earth-friendly, and requires less time).

If you've chosen the pressed-flower approach but have never pressed flowers, here are some instructions that should help:

──────── PRESSED FLOWERS FOR BEGINNERS ────────

There are many plant materials, including weeds and wildflowers, that retain their colors, shapes, and so on very well. As a general rule of thumb, plants with high water content aren't the best for pressing as they take much longer to dry and consequently are more susceptible to mold (which ruins the pressing).

Generally, pick your plants early in the day before the sun heats them up. This helps maintain color and some aroma (so your finished deck could even have a scent!). Lay your plants on several layers of newspaper to begin the drying process (just one day), then move them to an old phone book, leaving space between each plant and several pages of paper between each layer. Put a heavy object on top of the phone book so the flowers are literally squeezed. Typically it takes them two weeks to fully dry.

Once the plants are fully flat and dry, you can wax them as you would fall leaves (ironed between waxed paper, waxed sides in) before applying them to a surface. This seems to keep the more delicate pieces together longer. Glue each item where you want it on your card's surface, then either laminate or decoupage the set.

It's vital, once complete, that you store this deck in a dark space, as light will damage the color of the completed cards.

> **NOTE:** Rather than making a floral deck you can also put the flower pictures on wood slices for something that resembles a rune set. The only limitation here is that the size of the wood slices determines what type of plant part or picture you can utilize.

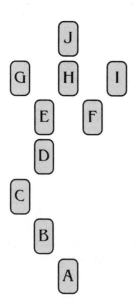

Once your cards have been completed, bless them and try them in various layouts. As with the other card systems, all the layouts for tarot work perfectly well, but you could also get somewhat creative here by looking more to nature for your layouts. For example, a four-card spread could relate to the elements of Earth, Air, Fire and Water. Or perhaps you could have a 10-card spread that looks like a flower when laid out like this:

When I use this layout, the spaces signify the following:

· **A:** The root of the question.

· **B:** People influencing the question (for boon or bane).

· **C:** Obstacles to overcome.

· **D:** The recent past that influences the present.

· **E:** What you have to work with—positives.

· **F:** Hopes and fears.

· **G:** Someone or something that provides help.

· **H:** Personal advice—central to the question.

· **I:** Your environment and its effects.

· **J:** The outcome card.

SAMPLE READING

The question: The relationship I'm currently in doesn't seem to be growing. Do we need to make changes or perhaps separate?

The reading: Say the outcome in a four card spread contained the Lilac, Primrose, Buttercup, and Violet cards. Lilac in the East signifies new love, meaning either this relationship is too young to make those kinds of leaps yet or that there's a new relationship on the horizon. Primrose in the South/Fire supports the idea that you haven't given this relationship enough of a chance. Buttercup in the West implies that your hopes, while positive, may be a little overzealous right now. However, the Violet in the North says both of you have all the devotion necessary to make a go of this.

Chapter 7

Cast Systems

> *Always remember that the future comes
> one day at a time.*
>
> —Dean Acheson

Cast systems are an old, venerable tradition. Castings are connected to the ancient custom of drawing lots, which is properly called *sortilege*, and appear in places as widely diverse as Samaria, Germany, Mesopotamia, Greece, and Oceana. Cast systems appeal to many people because there's no need to worry about the size and shape of your tokens; the casting system remains random because you literally toss the items on a surface.

People have used many different things for castings including:

- Bamboo sticks, in China (a system called *chim*).
- Beans, in Greece.
- Blocks, in China (called *Chiao Pai*).
- Bones and shells, in Far East, Roman, and Celtic cultures.

- ᚨ Yarrow stalks, in China (which became the *I Ching*).
- ᚨ Palm nuts, in Africa (called *Ifa*).
- ᚨ Pebbles or crystals, in various cultures (also known as *pessomancy*).
- ᚨ Runes, in Scandinavian and Germanic countries.

In some instances the items were tossed on a very specific surface that was either prepared ahead of time or drawn on the spot. In others, the diviner simply observed the entire casting and based the reading on traditional correlations, with no regard to the surface on which the tokens were cast. I personally prefer combining these two, that is, reviewing the whole outcome for patterns or clues, then breaking down the individual pieces. That's the approach I'm advocating with these homemade systems. And, don't forget that you could combine any of the cast systems with your divination boards.

Stones

In my travels, I've found that stones and crystals, compared to card systems, are far more forgiving of coffee, tea, and soda spills. Thus, I prefer my stone oracle to other less durable options—especially when I'm on the road. For those of you with children, this is an excellent choice for similar reasons. Kids are naturally attracted to pretty stones and love the tactile element, so it's also fairly easy to teach them how to use a set.

In determining what type of stones to include in your system you can look to the color and shape as a primary hint. For example, a pink-colored stone shaped like a heart would be an ideal token to represent matters of the heart (such as gentle love, or the love of a friend).

Alternatively, if you're going with crystals, consider their folkloric value. In this case, amethyst might represent self-control or balance because it was believed to keep a person from getting drunk in ancient times. Metaphysically amethyst represents peace, dreams, healing, and psychic energies.

As you assemble your stone set, gently appraise how each stone affects the others in the system. Do they "feel" right together? Do the system's energies blend well together? It took me about six months of mixing and matching stones to which I felt a strong attraction before I settled on the set that I've now used for 13 years. Because I'm very familiar with this set, I'll be using it for illustrative purposes.

I've chosen 14 stones and one central stone for my system. (I use a rutilated quartz for my central stone to disperse energy and as a "focal point" for the reading, but do not read a specific association for it.) Some of the stones have points so they can indicate the direction of specific energies or reveal something important, akin to a pointer. Some even look like eyes, which also adds greater dimension to the basic reading values. To this foundation I add a casting cloth that has the four directions, four seasons, and a Self/Now position in the center. Your casting surface can be anything you wish. I've just found this works well for me.

The positional values that correspond to my casting cloth are as follows:

- **North:** The new moon, quiet time, creating foundations, money, and physical matters.
- **Spring:** Wishes, fertility, growth, health.
- **East:** The waxing moon, beginnings, potential, excelling in something.
- **Summer:** Socialization, transformation, fervor, trials.
- **South:** The full moon, maturity, passion, endings.
- **Fall:** Harvest of labors, fulfillment, frugality.
- **West:** Waning moon, stricture, restraints, emotions, wisdom, intuition.
- **Winter:** Cooling (or slowing), rest, focus on hearth and home.
- **Self/Now:** Subjects that are intimate (close to you) or timely (now or very soon).

These place values then combine with the stone values. My set, which I chose both according to colors and shapes, as well as metaphysical associations, includes the following:

- **Amethyst:** Thankfulness; use of talents; self-healing; overcoming blockage.
- **Aventurine:** Living honestly and dependably; coincidences; money matters.
- **Brown agate:** Acceptance; balancing the ego; being responsible.
- **Carnelian:** Seeking the whole truth; improved sexual energy and emotions.
- **Cat's eye:** Perspective; prophetic insights; inner beauty; luck.
- **Citrine point:** Living compassionately; fears unfounded; improved sleep.
- **Eye agate:** Harmony or wholeness; stresses reduced; hearing the truth.
- **Fluorite:** Hope; the conscious mind; use of personal skills successfully.

· **Hematite:** Inner harmony; stability; renewal.

· **Lapis:** Walking the path of beauty with love and fidelity.

· **Malachite:** Being honest with yourself; business opportunity.

· **Moonstone**: Learning to give in order to receive; the psychic self; wisdom.

· **Rose quartz:** Service freely given; awareness of communications; clarity.

· **Turquoise:** Courage in times of trouble; travel or adventure.

SAMPLE READING

The question: A young woman came to me seeking a reading on the positive and negative underlying energies in her life.

The reading: She shook out just a few stones from my pouch onto the surface of the cloth. The turquoise landed between West and Winter, the malachite between Summer and Self, and brown agate landed nearly due center (Self/Now). This reading disturbed me because it seemed as if there was something very important this woman was overlooking. The Turquoise in that position often portended potential danger especially in travel. The malachite implied she wasn't seeing the danger. When I asked her about this, she explained that she'd been stalked by an ex-lover for about a week now (and had not gone to the police). Needless to say, the next thing I insisted upon was that she take action to protect herself (the brown agate's advice—be responsible!). Her previous relationship with this person had overcome common sense!

Dice

Divination by dice is called *cleromancy*. Homer alludes to the invention of dice around 1260 B.C.E. (at this point they were used to alleviate boredom on long sea voyages). Divination by dice was common in both Babylon and Assyria, the dice in this region being made from bone or clay. The number of dice that were used depends on the region. The Tibetan *So-mo*, for example, utilizes three dice, allowing for 16 values (from 3 to 18). Medieval Europeans rolled one die several times, and Victorian Americans seemed to prefer two dice (consulting this oracle on Monday or Wednesday).

To try cleromancy yourself, begin by drawing a circle on a piece of paper approximately 12 inches in diameter. Think of your question (keep it fairly simple), then roll three dice on that surface. Add together only those dice that land within the borders of the circle. Here are the traditional interpretive values to consider:

- **1:** Self; hermitage; time alone or downtime.
- **2:** Partnership; companionship; equity.
- **3:** Happy surprise or event.
- **4:** Troubles, obstacle, or unpleasant encounters.
- **5:** Fulfillment of hopes.
- **6:** Some type of loss or setback.
- **7:** Business or financial difficulties; undeserved slander.
- **8:** Misunderstandings (often due to communications).
- **9:** Unity; success; end to argument or problem.
- **10:** New beginning.
- **11:** Separation; moving away; distraction.
- **12:** Important news forthcoming.
- **13:** Sadness; depression; foreboding.

· **14:** Blossoming of a new friendship or partnership.

· **15:** Hold off on plans; ill-motivated people.

· **16:** Travel or adventure.

· **17:** Change your strategy or methods.

· **18:** Good fortune and victory.

SAMPLE READING

The question: An opportunity has presented itself for the querent to move elsewhere.

The reading: He or she rolls the dice and gets a 15. This would imply that this is not the best choice, and in fact the offer was likely made under highly dubious circumstances. On the other hand if the querent rolled and got a 10, that would be a very positive omen (or a "yes").

Dice-Casting Circle

To increase the potential meanings for cleromancy, you can segment your casting circle into 12 parts (similar to the spacing on a standard clock face). Label these spaces 1-12, each of which has a basic meaning such as:

· **1:** The future (this question isn't finished yet).

· **2:** Money issues.

· **3:** Movement.

· **4:** Home and family.

· **5:** Present or personally meaningful.

· **6:** Physical health.

· **7:** Relationships.

· **8:** Legal matters.

· **9:** Mental well-being.

· **10:** Job or career.

· **11:** Obstacles.

· **12:** Spiritual progress.

With those basics in place, you can choose to use only two dice this time for your reading (if you wish). In this case, consider the meaning of each number on the two die (if both dice land in the same section, add the numbers and use the association that corresponds to the *total*). Interpretive values are as follows:

· **1:** Yes or go ahead.

· **2:** No or stop.

· **3:** Be careful, but things are not as bad as you think.

· **4:** Consider your options carefully.

· **5:** Improved fortune; don't loose hope.

· **6:** Good sign for new projects.

· **7:** Faith will guide you (or instincts).

· **8:** Patience is necessary—don't rush.

· **9:** There's no need to wait!.

· **10:** Your doubts are well-founded.

· **11:** You already know the answer in your heart.

· **12:** Unlikely—reconsider your goals.

SAMPLE READING

The question: Again, the question regards whether or not moving is a good idea.

The reading: Let's say a one landed on the position of present, and a 9 landed on movement—this would be a *huge* "go ahead" signal. All the omens are very positive for this to be smooth and successful. On the other hand if both dice totaling 8 landed on obstacles, this implies you're rushing ahead too quickly. Pace your decision and consider it more carefully.

NOTE: You can get some really beautiful dice in various colors and styles at most toy or gaming stores. Some of these dice have more than 6 sides, which would allow you to create a system with increased interpretive values (just remember to write down the symbolic association for each number for consistency).

Salt Dough Runes

Salt dough is one of those wonderful items that seems to grow with your needs from childhood onward. It's very easy to make, color, and utilize, so it's a perfect media in which to design your own set of runes (or any other symbols that you'd like to carve into similarly sized and shaped tokens). Here's the basic recipe:

——————— MAKING SALT DOUGH ———————

- ∾ 1 cup table salt.
- ∾ 2 cups all-purpose flour.
- ∾ 1 Tbs. oil.
- ∾ 1/2+ cup cold water.

Mix salt and flour together with a spoon in a large bowl. Gradually add 1/2 cup water and the oil, and continue to mix. Keep adding water until you get a pie crust-like consistency. Once you can roll it into a ball, knead it on the table for a few minutes. Add another drop or two of water only if necessary for a consistent texture. At this juncture, if you wish to add food coloring to the blend, you can. Other ways to achieve color variations include:

- ∾ Using different types of flour.
- ∾ Adding spices (this makes for aromatic runes!).
- ∾ Painting, once dried.

Shape into whatever form you want for your finished runes, taking care to make them about the same size if you plan to use them for drawings as well. Carve the symbols you've chosen into each. These need to dry for 48 hours before you do anything else with them. Once they are completely dry, use fine sand paper to get rid of any rough edges. To protect the surface further, consider painting them and/or using a clear varnish or polyurethane.

So what symbols should you carve into your makeshift rune set? Well, certainly you could use traditional runes, but it's also fun to consider alternative emblems. For example, how about these:

&	Something additional that's needed but you've overlooked.
=	Balance, symmetry.
o	Cycles; the sun; protection and blessings.
X	You're right on target—keep your aim sure.
!	Pay attention, this is important.
+	What doesn't "add up" in this situation?
$	Money matters.
~	Iffy, uncertain.
?	Rethink your question.
^	Fire; passion; growing energy.
%	Stop dividing your interests or attentions.

NOTE: I just got these symbols from my keyboard, and I like them because I utilize those symbols all the time in daily work. Look for other common symbols that may have significance to you.

For your reference, the following are traditional runes and their correspondences:

ᛗ	Mannaz (M)	Inception; direction; maturity; modest change.
ᚷ	Gebo (G)	Service freely given; partnership and connection.
ᚨ	Ansuz (A)	Discussion; attention to counsel; paying attention to signs.
ᛟ	Othila (O)	Change in perspectives; hermitage or pilgrimage.
ᚢ	Uruz (U)	Gestation; slow, steady transformation; vitality.
ᛈ	Perth (P)	A surprise; initiation.
ᚾ	Nauthiz (N)	Frugality; limits; handling personal shadows.
ᛜ	Inguz (Ng)	Certainty; abundance; insight; lunar energy.
ᛇ	Eihwaz (E)	Forward-looking; proactiveness; overcoming.
ᛉ	Algiz (Z)	Personal honor; emotional balance; safety.
ᚠ	Fehu (F)	Fulfillment of goals and the ability to safeguard that accomplishment.
ᚹ	Wunjo (W)	Abundance; health; happiness.
ᛃ	Jera (J)	Completion and closure.
ᚲ	Kano (K)	Fire energy; openings.
ᛏ	Teiwaz (T)	Tenacity; the warrior.
ᛒ	Berkana (B)	Awareness; development.
ᛖ	Ehwaz (Eh)	Transition from one cycle or place to another; personal abilities.
ᛚ	Laguz (L)	Go with the flow; Water Element.
ᚺ	Hagalaz (H)	Freedom; new beginnings; creativity.
ᚱ	Raido (R)	Symmetry of many different energies; adventure or travel.
ᚦ	Thurisaz (Th)	Thoughtfulness and introspection; responsibility.
ᛞ	Dagaz (D)	Fulfillment; tremendous opportunity.
ᛁ	Isa (I)	The way; the self; potential blockage.
ᛋ	Sowelu (S)	Life energies at their fullest; sun energy.
	Odin (blank)	The unknowable; fate or destiny.

If you've made your runes of a similar size and shape (by the way, a cookie cutter works very well for that purpose), you can either cast them onto a surface or draw and lay them out like cards. If they are cast, those that land facedown would be disregarded, just as anything that lands off the casting surface. The sample reading provided here is based on a casting using the same type of cloth that I've described previously (on page 117).

SAMPLE READING

The question: I seem to be having a lot of bad luck. Is there something I should or could be doing to change things?

The reading: The "&" landed due East, meaning, to change things, first you must understand the patterns that brought you into this repetitive cycle. The "!" landed in the West, which implies your emotions have something to do with the problem (specifically either letting them lead you too much, or not enough). The last symbol to land on the cloth was the "%," between North and Self. This implies that at least part of your bad luck comes from a lack of focus. Pick one thing to fix, and follow through to the end.

Trash-to-Treasure Oracle

This is a really fun divination system that I created out of my proverbial "junk drawer." While I try to keep the pieces relatively small (for portability), you can really use anything if it's going to be cast on a surface. Some of the items I gathered (with potential interpretive values) include:

· **Battery (AA or AAA):** Energy levels.

· **Bolt:** Security; strong foundations.

· **Duct tape (piece):** Spirit; cohesiveness; balance.

· **Electrical tape:** Protection (especially from a shock).

· **Eraser:** Cleansing; a new start.

· **Glue stick:** Quick fixes.

· **Memory chip:** What are you forgetting?

· **Nail:** Hammering home your goals or wishes.

· **Nut:** An odd idea that just might work.

· **Paperclip:** Connections that prove important.

· **Pencil sharpener:** Get to the point!

· **Penny:** Luck, especially with money.

· **Screw:** Life's about to take a turn.

You can certainly use this system cast out on a surface like the other cast methods I've described. You could also close your eyes, think of a question, and just reach into a drawer full of goodies and see what your hand finds first!

SAMPLE READING

The question: Let's say you've experienced a bunch of technical problems lately—the microwave died, the freezer defrosted, the phone battery malfunctioned, and so on. You close your eyes and ponder: *Is this just circumstantial, or is there something else at work?*

The reading: The first thing your hand finds is a paperclip. That implies more is going on than meets the eye, and you might want to have your house wires checked (while also performing some protective magick)!

Chapter 8

Coins

I was taught very early that I would have to depend entirely upon myself; that my future lay in my own hands.

—Ogden Mills

The art of flipping coins as a way to help make a decision began in Rome and falls into the category of lot casting. At that juncture in history the Emperor was considered a type of deity, and his image on one side of the coin became the intermediary in difficult questions. Tradition tells us that the correct way to enact this ancient custom is by flipping the coin with your right hand, then placing it on the left hand to read the results (in plain view of all parties).

As a binary system, coins are best suited to very simple questions requiring nothing more than a yes/no, stay/go type of response. If you want more potential interpretive values, use several different coins to which you've assigned specific symbolic value. Heads is the positive interpretation of that value, and tails the negative. For example:

Coin	Association	Heads-up Meaning	Tails-up Meaning
Penny	Frugality (penny pinching).	Some constraints are easing.	Tighten your proverbial belt.
Nickel	Awareness.	Psychic insights are keen.	All is not what it seems; be wary.
Dime	Conservativeness.	You can be a little more liberal in your behavior.	Stick to your reserved nature.
Quarter	Elemental influences.	Energies working favorably.	Something is amiss.
Half dollar	Balance and equity.	Maintain a fair outlook.	Where have things become uneven or unfair?
Silver dollar	The moon's energies.	Trust your instincts.	Think rationally before acting.
Gold dollar	The sun's energies.	Blessings, hope, wholeness.	Reversal; loss.

NOTE: If you can't find the coins you want try painting or decorating tiddlywinks (the child's game) with suitable symbols and using them instead. It's an inexpensive alternative.

SAMPLE READING

The question: Should I join this coven?

The reading: Penny, heads; dime, tails; quarter, heads; half dollar, heads; silver dollar, tails; and gold dollar, heads. Overall, this is a very positive response. It implies that you should not try to be something you're not in your initial contacts with this group. Additionally, take your time and move slowly. There's no need to rush ahead until you feel fully comfortable.

Chapter 9

Dowsing

Every man is a hero and an oracle to somebody, and to that person whatever he says has an enhanced value.
—Ralph Waldo Emerson

The art of dowsing is technically called *rhabdomancy*, which covers the use of rods, wands, and twigs. The ancient Chinese, Turks, and Etruscans all dowsed for water, the latter frequently adding magickal incantations to the process. The Scythains utilized dowsing rods in their legal system in order to weed out truth from lies.

By the 1400s, people in England and Germany had adapted various methods of dowsing for finding ore, detecting criminals, analyzing character, curing disease, finding lost animals, tracing underground streams, finding the cardinal points, uncovering lost landmarks, and determining property lines. At this juncture, the earlier incantations had been replaced with Christian prayers, but the basic process remained the same, and the Church seemed to have no objections to it. In fact, we find a Friar Antonio in the mid-1500s dowsing to find water for St. Teresa of Spain who wanted to make sure of the proper placement for a convent!

Rods

Dowsing, also known as *water witching* because it was so often used in finding wells and other safe water sources, often employs forked branches or rods held in one's hands. It's interesting to note that even the U.S. Department of the Interior published a report on dowsing at the turn of the century—a time when oil companies were also employing dowsers to figure out where to drill. The theory of how dowsing works is fairly simple. The dowser becomes like a sonograph, using the forked branch like a needle. Interestingly enough, however, it seemed that at that point in history only about 10 percent of the population showed a talent for dowsing. Hopefully we're improving those numbers right now!

The favorite woods for dowsing rods were dogwood, peach, hazel, mulberry, juniper, maple, willow, and apple. In Tuscany, dowsers preferred almond, but when those weren't available a sprig of goldenrod or pomegranate branches were substituted. Any of these woods can be considered as potential dowsing rods, but really what's most important is that the twig is shaped like a capital Y.

Take a walk in a nearby forest or park and look for fallen branches. I don't recommend harvesting a branch unless you feel strongly drawn to a particular tree's spirit (and don't forget to leave an offering afterward). You're looking for a branch of about 14–18 inches, with a neck of about 4–11 inches. Once you find one, you'll want to clean it up and bless it.

With the rods I collect, I carefully remove the bark using a wood awl and then gently sand the surface so as to not get splinters using it. After that I periodically treat the wood with lemon oil, which you can buy at nearly any supermarket shelved with cleaning products. This keeps the wood from cracking over time.

Using the Rod

Using this tool is a little different than the other readings we've discussed thus far because its function is unique. This tool traditionally is one utilized for *finding* something, as opposed to *answering* specific questions. Using it is pretty simple.

Hold each side of the forked part of the branch in your hands, keeping the third extension parallel to the ground. Now begin walking, focusing on what it is you wish to find. For example, think about locating a lay line or vortex and walk for a while. When the branch tugs downward, mark that spot. Now move back and walk toward that region again to see if the same thing occurs (most dowsers check their results three times). If it does, you'll want to walk out from that point in several directions to see if it's a line of energy or just a small bundle. This is a great activity if you're looking for a place in which to hold a gathering, to work a special spell, or to meditate where the energies are high and uplifting. It's also how the ancients often determined the placement for their temples and other sacred sites!

NOTE: New Age stores often sell dowsing kits constructed from thin, metal, L-shaped rods. The small leg of the rod is held in each hand while you're walking an area. When the two rods cross at the center, this is considered a "hit." The price typically ranges from $15–40. If that's too expensive, you can make a similar set for free out of two L-shaped branches of similar size, or bend two thin bars of metal (which you can likely get at a hardware store for far less than $15).

Pendulums (With Symbol Sets)

The Romans appear to be the first people to use pendulums for divination, specifically to determine the outcome of planned battles. The pendulum wasn't always observed by itself. Sometimes it was used a bit like a Ouija board in that it was placed above a circle of letters so it could spell out responses. This means that you can potentially utilize your own pendulums in conjunction with the board systems or casting cloths you've made as part of other projects thus far.

The pendulum can be used for dowsing, but it was also employed in answering simple questions or determining names. For example, among the Koryak, the father of a newborn child used a pendulum to find out what relative had been reincarnated in the child. When the pendulum moved quickly, that was an affirmative response and the child was often given that relative's name.

Other applications for a pendulum include locating a region of disease, finding items, uncovering polarities, and seeking out power centers. Down through history, many objects have been used as pendulums including a spiral seashell, bundles of herbs, and wedding rings. However, experts in this art claim that the best base material for pendulums is brass, amber, silver, or copper strung on wool, cotton, or linen. This frugal Kitchen Witch, while wishing to honor history, says "Bah" to all that fanciness. It's simply not cost effective, unless you happen to have an evenly weighted item handy in one of those medias, so I'm going to suggest two options.

The first is the use of a personal ring. This approach was popular in the middle ages, and known by the term *dactylomancy*. At this juncture, the type of ring was chosen according to the day of the week for best results. Questions posed on Sunday required a gold and peridot ring; Monday, silver and quartz; Tuesday, iron and ruby; Wednesday, tin with carnelian; Thursday, tin with topaz; Friday, copper and emerald; and Saturday, lead with onyx. While this is fairly impracticable today, I have seen some shops carry solid stone rings that are very inexpensive, so that might be one way to go.

Another more simple approach is using any ring you have handy (if you wear it a lot, you may wish to cleanse it first). To personalize things a little more, coordinate the color of the string with your question (such as using red thread for love or green thread for money matters). If the ring has a stone in it, make sure that stone is suspended downward like a pointer from a good length of string (at least slightly longer than the distance from the tip of your middle finger to your elbow).

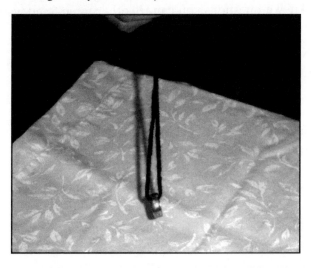

The second media I like to use for pendulums is herbs or plants. My reasoning is simple: These items have metaphysical properties that we associate with them. You can choose the herb/plant according to your question similarly to choosing the color of your string.

For example, if asking about health, you might use a bundle of thyme or marjoram (both of which are used to maintain well-being). This choice provides your efforts with improved sympathetic energy, and therefore should hone the results. As with the ring, you want to tie the herb bundle or plant into the string in such a way as to create an even balance so it swings smoothly.

Once the ring or herb bundle is secured, hold the end of the string between the thumb and index finger of your writing hand, so that the ring rests just above a flat surface (not touching the surface). Begin your experiments with simple questions to which you know the answer. For example, ask the pendulum if you're a male. Clockwise movement by the pendulum is a "yes" while counter clockwise is a "no." When you achieve a high level of success with known questions you can try other topics, and watch for specific movements in the pendulum as follows:

- **North/South movements:** Positive; yes; go ahead.
- **East/West movement:** Negative; no; stop.
- **Circle:** Harmony; joy; improved energy. (The larger the circle, the better.)
- **Bobbing:** Uncertainty; misinformation; wait.
- **Ellipse:** Lack of clarity; communication problems; duality.
- **Ellipse East/West:** Great love; sensitivity; emotion.
- **Ellipse North/South:** Strong feminine instincts.
- **Ellipse diagonal:** Depression; deceit; ethical issues.
- **Strong vertical strokes (off center):** Ego and dominance.
- **Strong horizontal strokes (off center):** Physical drive.
- **Jerky motion in strokes:** Sickness or disease.
- **Diagonal strokes:** Conflict; obstacles.

SAMPLE READING

The question: Will this seasonal job continue longer than expected?

The reading: The pendulum responded by first moving up and down on a strong North/South line, but then became slightly diagonal. The basic interpretation would be that there's potential for more work, but not without some issue that must be overcome.

Chapter 10

Drawn Systems

*We often discover what will do, by finding
out what will not do; and probably he who
never made a mistake never made a
discovery.*

— Samuel Smiles

As you review various drawn systems, you'll notice that
the media are either of very similar sizes and shapes, or
incredibly diversified. With those of a similar size and
shape, a reader will often close his or her eyes and touch
each token, waiting for some type of sensual cue that indicates the token in his or her hand is the "correct" one for
pulling. He or she then places the token in some type of
spread as you might a tarot deck.

With drawn systems that are highly diversified, the
reader does not touch the items, but holds his or her hand
palm down toward the tokens. The reason for this is simple.
If one were to touch the tokens, the subconscious awareness of particular tokens and their meanings might skew
the reading. Nonetheless, the reader is still waiting for some
type of gut-level cue to determine where to put his or her

hand down and pick up tokens. These also are typically laid out in a spread, unless the question is one of a very simple nature.

It's interesting to note that some cast systems such as runes and sticks were also sometimes drawn. Thus we get the familiar image of a group of people huddling around a handful of sticks drawing out one that determines their fate (the short stick typically being a bad thing). This is how we come by the expression "getting the short end of the stick!"

Dominoes

Divination by dominoes is a form of *cleromancy*. It originated in China around the 12th century B.C.E. Originally there were 32 in a set (as opposed to the modern 28), decorated with red spots instead of white. Another version of dominoes originated in Alaska, where 148 pieces were used.

Practitioners of this system recommend consulting it no more than once a week, and to avoid readings on Monday or Friday, which are not considered auspicious. Begin by laying all the dominoes facedown on a table and shuffling them. Draw one while thinking of a simple question. The traditional interpretive values follow:

- **Double 6:** Omen of luck, prosperity, and happiness.
- **6/5:** Good for relationships or social situations.
- **6/4:** Arguments; negative outcomes in legal matters.
- **6/3:** An adventure or travel.
- **6/2:** Overall improvements.
- **6/1:** The end of a problem (thanks to generosity or kindness).

· **6/blank:** Caution; gossip.

· **Double 5:** Transformation and movement; possible new job or home.

· **5/4:** An unexpected windfall.

· **5/3:** A meeting with an authority figure goes well.

· **5/2:** Difficulties in a relationship or partnership.

· **5/1:** Being busy.

· **5/blank**: An ending or closure; caution with money.

· **Double 4:** Celebrations; smooth progress.

· **4/3:** Worries that are unfounded.

· **4/2:** Career or financial changes; watch contracts.

· **4/1:** Firm relationships but shaky finances.

· **4/blank:** Disappointment or bad news.

· **Double 3:** Abundance; sudden change in a working relationship.

· **3/2:** A bad time to take risks.

· **3/1:** Important discoveries; slander.

· **3/blank:** Arguments at home or with friends.

· **Double 2:** Jealousy has something to do with this question.

· **2/1:** Bad time for financial dealings (avoid the market).

· **2/blank:** Reconsider this move or partnership.

· **Double 1:** Good fortune comes from an odd place.

· **1/blank:** Unexpected guests.

· **Double blank:** a very bad omen; trouble for which you're unprepared.

SAMPLE READING

The question: I feel like people are taking advantage of my good nature. Is this true?

The reading: (For a past, present, and future layout spread) past, double 2; present, 4/3; future, 6/1. This layout might be interpreted as saying that in the past there were times people misused your kind-hearted nature. Today, however, that no longer seems to be true. Don't look for trouble where there isn't any. In terms of the future, it seems someone is about to renew your faith in others—especially friends.

Garden Guru

During the Victorian era and even before then, farmers and gardeners might go to their fields and randomly pick a plant while thinking of a question. Whatever item came into their hands provided the answer in symbolic form (according to the language of flowers discussed in Chapter 6, on page 110). Technically this was called *florimancy* and it's but one of several forms of divination that utilizes flowers. Another comes from Greece, in which a petal corresponding to the question was placed in the bottom of a bowl. The querent would voice his or her question while the bowl was filled with water. If the petal rose, the omen was positive (or a "yes"). Here are just a few more flowers and their interpretive values to consider if you have a garden handy in which to turn to nature's language for insights:

· **Aloe:** Good luck.

· **Bachelor button:** A true and trustworthy companion.

· **Clover:** Charm.

· **Daffodil:** Improved money.

· **Daisy:** Love.

· **Dandelion:** Prophetic or psychic insights.

· **Geranium:** Guests soon to arrive.

· **Lilac (five petal):** Serendipity in abundance.

· **Pansy:** Hopes and fears.

· **Roses:** Romance.

· **Shepherd's purse (green seed pod):** Financial loss.

If you don't have a garden, you can still assemble a drawn system based on these flowers and those listed previously (on page 110). Try decoupaging the actual petals (if you can get them) or a picture on wooden squares or craft paper. Alternatively, wax the flowers with an iron, between squares of waxed paper (each of these needs to be of a similar size and shape). This latter option won't be as durable, but it is fast and simple for those moments when you're challenged for time.

In terms of readings, you can pull just one symbol or several, depending on how much detail you want/need. If pulling more than one, lay them out in a spread, each position of which has a predetermined theme akin to the tarot or the Victorian floral cards discussed in Chapter 6. (You can also refer to that section for a sample reading.)

Rods 'n' Reason

Hosea 4:12 reads, "...and their rods give them oracles." That gives you some idea of just how long people have been utilizing the art of divination by rods. The rod represents leadership and authority, which is likely why they first appeared in divinatory systems.

Saxon tradition had a seven-rod system made from wood. There were three short pieces and four long, only one of the latter having special decorations. The long, decorated rod was placed along a north/south axis as the querent focused on his or her question and released the remaining rods to fall on the north-south indicator (resembling Pick Up Sticks in some ways).

For the purpose of your homemade rod system, we're going to begin with eight flat sticks of wood or, if you prefer, some sturdy cardboard. The sticks need not be any larger than about 3 inches long and 1/2 inch wide, but you may want to make them a bit bigger for ease of handling. Now paint the sticks, four with one dot in the middle, and the other four with a dot on each end. (You'll be drawing four of them, so this creates 16 potential patterns.)

Turn the sticks upside down before you. Close your eyes and shuffle them, then (with your eyes open) draw four of the sticks and place them side by side horizontally (long sides facing you), to form a rectangle. Turn the sticks upright to reveal the pattern of the dots. The arrangement provides you with interpretive values, as follows:

A path laid before you; possible travel or opportunity; movement; action.

A new start; be aware and alert; keep your duties wisely balanced; trust yourself.

The Goddess; nurturing, insight, and improved relationships with women.

Luck, victory, blessings; karmic return threefold.

God; strength, leadership, and the necessity to harness the masculine energies within.

Gains, advancement, improvement—especially with money.

Obstacles; a closed door; life on hold; negative emotions holding back positive action; doubt.

Sadness; hopes crushed; unexpected loss or disappointment.

Decline or setback; prepare bravely to meet adversity.

Unity, love, kinship, or friendship; overall beneficial unions.

Technical troubles, red tape; conflict causing misunderstanding.

Be patient and tenacious; keep an even pace—moderation in all things.

A joyful bit of serendipity or success (often a result of honesty or honorable action).

 Too much emotion and not enough logic—take some time to sort out your thoughts and heal.

 In the tarot, this corresponds to the sun—that is, all good things! Carpe diem and find fulfillment.

 People in and around your life and the messages or lessons they provide—listen!

SAMPLE READING

The question: Is my lover being faithful?

The reading: The symbol assembled is one that indicates too much emotion in play. Perhaps you and your mate have recently argued or found yourself on inequitable ground. That can easily taint your perspectives. Before jumping to conclusions and making hurtful accusations, think this through with a clear head.

Chapter 11

Dream Aids

*Dream manfully and nobly, and thy
dreams shall be prophets.*
　　　　　　—Edward G. Bulwer-Lytton

The great Arab historian Ibn Khaldun was once quoted as saying, "dream vision is an awareness in the part of the rational soul in its spiritual essence; a glimpse of the forms of events." He was certainly not alone in his opinion or in his writings. Plato wrote that the sleeping mind shared warnings and perspectives through a dream, Mohammed trusted in his dreams to guide him, and the writings of Caesar and Tacitus recite the German and Celtic regard for dreaming true (prophetic dreams). It seems that people around the world—including the leaders of Samaria, Mesopotamia, Egypt, Israel, and Japan—all respected night visions as being profoundly meaningful.

The oldest surviving dream book dates to 1350 B.C.E., in which the meanings of various images appearing in a person's dreams were detailed in nearly modern terms. Later, dream books circulated liberally in Greece around 400 B.C.E., and Romans developed special rituals for interpreting prophetic dreams. Of them, the *Oneirocritica* by Artemidorus (C.E. 140) continues to be consulted by those interested in this field of study.

Some of the most detailed dream rituals come to us from Japan. Around the 4th or 5th century C.E. the Japanese Emperor communed with the supernatural world in his role as the official dreamer for the nation. This required certain periods of isolation in a specially built Hall of Dreams. Not surprisingly, this increased the popularity of dream interpretation around the country, and it remained fairly acclaimed until around the 15th century.

It's interesting to note that some of the ritualistic over-tones for receiving visionary dreams are ones we could try utilizing too. For example, it was recommended that a person abstain from meat or strong vegetables, and make an offering or prayers to Deity. After this, the querent was to wait inside the temple a specific number of days to receive his or her dream. Oddly, the dream typically came at the very last day, so perhaps Spirit was trying to teach our ancestors patience! In any case, the idea of adjusting our diets, and using prayer (or perhaps meditation) as one way of unlocking prognosticative dreams still has merit. Each person is different, but I find having a light snack (nothing complex or spicy) helps improve the sleep cycle so dreams are more likely to go uninterrupted.

The number of dream harbingers and the diversity of interpretations are fairly astounding if you review global writings. To try and cover them all in a book of this nature would prove cumbersome, not to mention difficult due to the subjective nature of dreams. Rather, I would like to suggest that you find one or two books on dream interpre-tation to utilize along with these dreaming aids. This way you have tools through which to motivate divinatory dreams, and a way of understanding them afterward!

Dream Sachet

One way to improve your ability to receive and remember dreams is by using magickal aromatherapy. Incense and scented candles would fit the bill, but it's not safe to leave something burning while you sleep. A perfect substitute, then, and one that you can keep under your pillow is a dream sachet.

To make this you'll need a 4-inch square of natural fabric. Choose a color that you associate with dreams. Into the center of that fabric place some rose petals, marigold petals, jasmine oil (if available), and perhaps a small quartz crystal to energize the blend. Tie this up tightly using string or yarn. As you tie the string you may wish to add an incantation such as:

> With the knot of one this spell's begun.
> With the knot of two, bring dreams–true.
> With the knot of three, night visions to me!
> With the knot of four, I open the door.
> With the knot of five, the magick's alive.
> So be it.

Put this under your pillow on any night when you have a pressing question in mind, or when you'd like to have a spiritually significant dream.

As an aside, it's perfectly acceptable to undertake dreaming inside the parameters of a sacred space. Just cast your circle around, above, and below your bed. Like the dream catcher that follows, this helps filter the dream imagery so you get what you most need.

Dream Catcher

The idea of a dream catcher originates in Native American tradition. Typically they're made from grape vines (or some other type of flexible wood), sinew, crystals, and feathers. The idea is that the intricate weaving of the dream catcher, which looks a lot like a spider web, catches any bad dreams and attracts the good ones.

I have found a lovely way to adapt this idea that will save you a little time and still provide a functional and visually pleasing dream catcher. To make it you'll need some beads (preferably wood or crystal—not plastic), feathers, ribbon, a lacy doily, and (if you wish) silk flowers or other small decorations. Each one, however, should be somehow symbolic of your goal, namely dreaming. For example you might gather together a white feather for protection, yellow ribbon (for divinatory energy), amethyst crystals (for peaceful sleep), and azurite pieces (for dreaming).

Once you gather your components, take a moment to bless them saying something such as:

> Come sleep of night where starlight teems,
> Bring to me prophetic dreams.

Next, lay out the doily and set your various components thereon. Move them around until you find a pleasing configuration. Then stitch or glue each item in its place. Last, but not least, hang it on a wall above your bed.

A final piece of advice: Keep a dream journal or taped log. Make your records first thing upon waking so the memories are fresh. If you get more details later, record those too. As you review the notes, bear in mind that the meaning of many dreams will not become clear until days or weeks (and in the case of prophetic dreams, even years) later. I suggest reading over or listening to your notes about once every three months to see what things have manifested, and what new insights can be gained.

Dreamy Foods

Many ancient texts allude that eating various foods just prior to going to bed improves one's chances of receiving a spiritual or predictive dream. This is probably why we often joke about some dreams being the result of pizza or other spicy foods. In any case, should you wish to try adding various foods into your diet to see if they help you, onions, raisins, and rice are three items mentioned in German, Scottish, and Chinese tradition respectively. Note, however that the rice was mixed with lychee fruit, cherries, dates, plums, diced lotus flower, cinnamon, ginger, and orange—a blend which not only improves psychic abilities but brings visionary dreams.

Chapter 12

Household Omens and Signs

In today already walks tomorrow.
　　　　　—Samuel Taylor Coleridge

The law of cause and effect is something we've been taught since we were children. That was not the case for our most ancient ancestors who had nothing but observation to help them understand what we now consider everyday knowledge. And, of course, they observed their personal environment the most closely, hoping to prepare for whatever the fates portended. This is omen observation—the careful scrutiny of specific occurrences or objects watching for prescribed trends. Any observation that proved correct more than once was often passed down as a "truth."

For the purpose of this book we're going to look at some of the signs and omens that await you right in your sacred space of home. The beauty of this divinatory approach is threefold. First, you only need to keep your senses sharp to pick up the omens and signs. Second, because this method centers around your personal living area, it tends to respond more personally. And third, the truly clever Kitchen Witch can use many of these bits of lore as the foundation for spells, charms, rituals, or whatever. Here are just a few for your consideration:

- **Apron:** Putting your apron on backward portends good fortune. If your day's been lousy, you might want to take an apron or any piece of clothing and turn it inside out to likewise "turn" the energy around!

- **Ashes:** If you have a fireplace, watch for patterns in the soot of the fire (or follow the guidelines for pyromancy and observe the movements of the flames).

- **Birds:** A bluebird on your windowsill tells of joy to follow. Crows cawing nearby speak of ill winds. Seeing an eagle out your window brings a hope to fruition, and a hummingbird speaks of fidelity and devotion among those who dwell in the house. Red birds appearing suggest a wish coming true, and hearing a wren's song means your prospects are improving.

- **Bread:** As a staple, burning bread or wasting it was considered a bad omen, especially for finances. With this in mind, breadcrumbs might make an excellent prosperity or providence component. Share some with the birds and let your questions fly on their wings.

- **Broom:** Finding a broom in a new residence speaks of good luck. To keep that fortune going, always sweep toward the center of a room to keep luck from going out the door.

- **Cat:** If you notice your cat washing itself in a doorway, prepare for an honored visitor. If a cat abandons your home, it's a very negative sign (move with the cat!). Stray cats coming in of their own will is a positive sign, and a cat that enters the room where you sit right paw first brings improved fortune with him or her.

· **Coffee:** If you find bubbles in your coffee, money will arrive soon.

· **Dish rag:** If you drop a dish rag, it means something special is about to happen.

· **Dog:** A howling dog means bad things for the person first hearing it, especially in partnerships. A dog coming into the house and lying near your bed portends new possessions.

· **Drinking glass:** To accidentally make a glass ring means someone is literally or figuratively drowning. To turn that negative energy around, quickly stop the ringing by touching the rim of the glass.

· **Egg:** An egg accidentally breaking on the floor predicts forthcoming news.

· **Knife:** Dropping a knife and having it land with its point sticking into the ground is a good sign for the day.

· **Oil:** Spilling oil while preparing dinner predicts improvements, especially in business.

· **Pin:** A pin dropped and discovered on your kitchen floor implies you're going to be traveling soon. If the head faces toward you, expect a pleasant vacation.

· **Salt:** Salt spilled on the table indicates there are spirits nearby. Pick the salt up and toss it over your shoulder to banish them. (Note that salt is regularly used in magick for cleansing and protection.)

· **Tea:** Finding bubbles in your tea speaks of an unexpected guest's arrival.

- **Utensils:** Two knives accidentally crossing on the table predict an argument or conflict. The crossing of a knife and fork represents hostility aimed toward you. Dropping a spoon in the kitchen tells of a woman guest arriving, a fork, a male guest, and a knife, a youthful guest.
- **Wood:** Accidentally hitting your hand against a piece of wood is a good omen for love.

I'm sure many of these seem quaint and charming to our modern eyes, but it's not difficult to see where the connections between folkways and magick still often remain strong (salt being but one good example). The beauty of folkways is that no one thinks of them as remotely "witchy"—just something we follow because they work! This comfort zone makes a lot of these tidbits very functional for everyday spiritual needs with the least amount of fuss.

Chapter 13

Food Findings

Food probably has a very great
influence on the condition of men.
Wine exercises a more visible influence,
food does it more slowly but perhaps just
as surely. Who knows if a well-prepared
soup was not responsible for the pneu-
matic pump or a poor one for a war? .

—Georg Christoph Lichtenberg

You knew I'd eventually get around to food, didn't you? I often joke with family and friends that, as a Kitchen Witch, it's my solemn duty to turn anything magickal into a food group (then eat it, of course!). In the case of divination, it seems I wasn't alone in this goal. Our ancestors used a variety of foods to foretell the future. Let's explore several options that are easily adaptable to modern living.

Bread

Divination using bread is properly referred to as *alphitomancy*. When bread was tossed into water, and floated, it was believed the weather would be calm. Bread falling butter-side (or jelly-side) down on the floor implies forthcoming guests. If you bake two loaves of bread together and they join, it's a sign of a good union. If you cut bread unevenly, watch your communications throughout that day. Finally, if bread crumbles in your hand beware of arguments.

Coffee

The art of reading remnant coffee grounds found in one's cup very likely owes its origin to tea leaf reading, and may have evolved around the 18th century, when coffee began to find popular acceptance in Italy. Now, for those of you who are not coffee drinkers—have no fear. You need not drink a cup of coffee for this system to work for you.

Begin by dampening the inside of a white cup. Hold a heaping teaspoon of coffee grounds in your strong hand and think of a question. Sprinkle this into the cup, give it a good shake, and then turn it over—tapping the bottom lightly to eliminate loose grounds. Look inside the cup now, checking for shapes. A shape that appears close to the edge of your  cup speaks of timely matters, while those in the bottom talk of the future.

Following are a few patterns and their common values. If this list isn't sufficient, utilize the one for tea leaves on pages 169-172 (or any good book of symbolism that you have handy), when the meaning eludes you.

· **Anchor:** Hope; success in business. At the bottom of the cup, an anchor implies firm foundations especially in relationships.

· **Bird:** If in an area of the cup uncluttered by grounds, you can expect troubles to clear up soon. When a bird seems to be flying through an area thick with grounds, anticipate that an upcoming journey will be successful.

· **Cross:** Near the rim, this speaks of troubles soon coming to an end (often on the heels of making a decision).

· **Dog:** Faithful friends, especially when near the rim of the cup. Toward the bottom, however, it may imply a jealous friend (or a misunderstanding between friends).

· **Flower:** Discovering an unexpected talent or skill and being successful with it.

· **House:** Blessings, especially when nearer the rim of the cup. At the bottom it portends vigilance as the key to success.

· **Leaf or clover:** Good luck. However, if the leaf appears in a cluttered area of the coffee grounds, it implies that luck is overshadowed by some difficulties.

· **Lily:** Near the rim, this speaks of pure virtue. However, if it appears across from you be forewarned that someone isn't being honest.

· **Moon:** Honor. If it appears in a cluttered area, those honors come with momentary sadness.

· **Mountain:** Favor with an authority figure.

- **Rings:** Cycles in relationships. Clouded rings warn of deception. A ring at the bottom of a cup speaks of being separated from someone you love.
- **Roads:** Movement and transformation. Those dotted with grounds also speak of improved finances along the way. Smudged roads warn of reversals or halted movement.
- **Star:** Longevity for a person or project.
- **Tree:** Personal health, if the tree is crisp and clear. If cloudy or in a cluttered region, take care with your health.

SAMPLE READING

The question: I'm thinking of getting out of the business I'm in and using transferable skills to find a new job. Will this effort be successful?

The reading: An uncluttered star toward the bottom of the cup, a flower near the rim. The flower is a definite "yes" to the question at hand, as is the star. However, because the star is at the bottom of the cup, you should anticipate success taking some time, probably months.

As an aside, I know people who also scry their coffee creamer. To utilize this method, pour in about a tablespoon full of cream, and stir it once clockwise while focusing on your question. The patterns that appear in the cream can be interpreted similarly to those in the grounds. And if you like the reading's outcome, go ahead and drink the coffee to internalize that positive energy!

Beans

The ancient Greeks used black and white beans as a binary system of divination. For this, an equal number of each color bean was used along with a deep, opaque vase and a piece of lead. The querent would drop in the beans, hold the lead piece while thinking of his or her question, then drop it in and shake the vessel. The diviner (typically a Priestess) would retrieve the lead and one bean. A black one meant no, while the white bean meant yes or a positive omen.

This system is perfectly apt (akin to flipping a coin) for yes or no answers. You may, however, want to use a crystal or some other durable item as a substitute for a piece of lead (which is a toxic element). To improve the potential reading values, begin with the basic Greek method, pulling the token plus one bean. You now have the yes or no indicator. To clarify this, remove all but one each of the black and white beans. Next, put beans of similar sizes but different colors into the jar. Think of your question again and pull out one more bean with the token. In this case, your clarifier here is based on the hue, which provides the underlying keynote for your question:

· **Yellow:** Communication or logic.

· **Green:** Growth (maturity) or money.

· **Brown:** Foundations or security.

· **Red:** Love or health.

· **Black:** Negativity or foreboding.

· **White:** Spirit's influence or purity.

SAMPLE READING

The question: Money is very tight. Will things improve soon?

The reading: Beans pulled are white and yellow. The basic response here is yes, things will improve, but it's going to require that you communicate your needs, and make logical plans on how to fix things mundanely.

Cheese

A system called *tironmancy* probably originated in Greece or Rome. First it was simply the observation of milk as it curdled, looking for specific symbols in the final formation. Later, a block of cheese was sliced and the holes counted to determine either how the days or weeks ahead fared (an even number being a positive omen) or how long it would take before a certain situation or wish manifested. In the latter case, the total of the holes indicated the response in days, weeks, months, or possibly years. If you decide to try this yourself, bear in mind that the larger the holes are in the cheese (I suggest using Swiss for obvious reasons), the more momentous the events in store.

Corn

Divination using corn appeared in two different forms in Mexico. In the first system, a reader would place 30 kernels of corn in a bowl. The querent would focus on his or her question and scoop up a random number of kernels. The kernels removed from the bowl were then divided into groups of four, as were those remaining in the bowl. If the querent's selected kernels and those left in the bowl both yielded an even number of piles, with possible leftover kernels, the omen was favorable. An odd number of piles from both groups of kernels, with possible leftovers, was unfavorable. A mixed outcome (one even number of piles and one odd number of piles) revealed something hidden or unknown about the question at hand. The fewer leftover kernels, the more intense the omen; no leftovers indicated a strong prediction. You can try this yourself using popcorn kernels. If you get a positive omen, use those kernels in a special luck-drawing charm, or perhaps pop and eat them to digest your good fortune completely!

The second method entailed a querent going before an image of the god Quetzalcoatl to petition him for insights. Here, the question was voiced and the kernels scattered on the ground before him. If the corn landed evenly spread out, it was a positive omen. Mind you, each person's perspective of "even" makes this a subjective system at best. If you decide to try it, I would suggest utilizing a statue of a personal deity.

Egg

Divination using eggs, called *ovoscopy* or *oomantia*, was popularized around the 1600s in Europe. One method begins with poking a hole in the small end of a raw egg. Holding this over a glass of water, you ponder your question then interpret the patterns formed by the egg as it drops on the surface (akin to the patterns in coffee creamer or tea leaves).

The second approach uses colored eggs, which might be best undertaken during the Spring Equinox, or you could simply color the shells of the eggs emptied out in the first method. (Plastic colored eggs can also be used—they'll last forever and you can put tolkens inside for more interpretive value!) You'll need seven different colored eggs in a deep bowl. Think of your question and blindly choose one. The interpretive values follow:

- **Red:** Activity, a warning, or arguments.
- **Orange:** Unavoidable transition; rewards reaped for hard work.
- **Yellow:** Think before you act; don't wholly trust your emotions.
- **Green:** Inventiveness; the muse; personal growth.
- **Blue:** Peace of mind; good relationships.
- **Pink:** Improved prospects; friends.
- **Undyed:** Fate; the unknowable.
- **Mixed:** Confusion or multiple options.

SAMPLE READING

The question: I'd like to invest in a specific stock. Is this a good time?

The reading: The egg pulled is Yellow. This is a cautionary color that indicates the time isn't right. If you need more clarification, think of what you want to know (like should I invest in that stock later?) and pull a second egg. If, in this case, you get the undyed egg it means there are too many variables.

Flour

Aleuromancy originated in Greece at the temples for Apollo. Here the priestess sprinkled flour on water and scried the pattern it created. Alternatively, small pieces of paper with "fortunes" written on them were wrapped in flour dough balls, somewhat like an ancient fortune cookie. The only difference is that the flour ball was placed in water in a bowl then drawn out at random.

If you'd like to make some fortune cookies as a party favor, or even to use more seriously during times such as

Samhain (which are considered good for divinatory efforts) the first step is to write up fortunes using non-toxic ink. The best size for furtunes is 1/2 inch wide by about 2 inches long. I suggest an even number of positive, negative, and somewhat neutral words. For example, a positive fortune might read "Yes, go for it!" A negative one could be "Wait or stop; this isn't a good time." A neutral example is "Be cautious—check your options first."

The next step, of course, is baking the cookies. Here's a recipe:

FORTUNE COOKIES

Yield: 8 cookies. Prep time: about 1 hour.

- ৯৯ 1 large egg white.
- ৯৯ 1/4 cup all-purpose flour.
- ৯৯ 1/4 cup sugar.
- ৯৯ 1/2 tsp. five spice powder.
- ৯৯ 1/4 cup finely chopped almonds.
- ৯৯ Fortunes.

Directions: Begin by preheating your oven to 400 degrees. Meanwhile butter a goodly portion of a baking sheet (about a 6-inch round area). In a bowl, hand whisk the egg white until it's foamy. Add the dry ingredients and beat until smooth. Place two teaspoons of batter on the buttered area of the baking sheet and spread it out smoothly so it measures about 3 inches. If there's enough room you can do two or three on a sheet, but you'll have to fold them quickly when they're warm so don't *bake* too many at once.

Bake these for about 5 minutes, until golden brown around the edges of the cookie. Remove the cookies from the sheet and invert them while still hot. Put the fortune folded in the middle, then fold the cookie in half. Bend the pointed edges of the cookie toward each other so they hook. Let these cool and start on your next batch. This recipe only makes about 8 cookies, so you may need to double it to get a wide variety of fortunes. Store in an airtight container.

Hints: Use more than one baking sheet for this recipe to make the process go faster. A good way to shape the cookies is by wrapping them around a bowl or measuring cup.

Oil

The tradition of *lecanomancy*, or divination by oil, comes to us from the Middle East, specifically Babylon. Lecanomancy was often a family practice, handed down through the generations. To begin, the diviner sits cross-legged in front of a bowl of water while pondering a question. They then add oil and interpret the movement on the surface of the water as follows:

- **Dividing:** A negative omen; separation or an argument.
- **Ring:** Profit, recovery, or safety.
- **Droplets:** Fertility or prosperity.
- **Thin, even covering:** Trouble ahead or clouded perspectives.
- **Crescent or star:** Good fortune.
- **One large drop and one small:** Health, renewal, or birth.

In trying this yourself, you could perhaps add food coloring to the water in a hue that represents the focus of your question. Overall, clockwise movement is positive, and counterclockwise negative. You might also look for specific shapes as you would with coffee and tea readings.

SAMPLE READING

The question: I've felt a distance between a friend and myself. Is there a problem here?

The reading: (Based on traditional symbolic values) at first the oil divides, but then it begins to swirl clockwise. This would indicate some type of mis-understanding has separated the two of you, but you still have a chance to make things right. Think about what happened and give him or her a call!

Onions

It's uncertain as to where divination with onions began. Some people believe it was Egypt, where the onion was regarded as a symbol of the universe. In Germany, however, we find some written records that tell us how to use this vegetable for prognostication.

The first approach is to plant several onions, one per pot. Each pot represents one possible outcome to your question (it's best to label them so you remember which is which). In determining potential outcomes it's important to be balanced. Have at least one positive, one negative, and one neutral container. For example, if you're asking a question about the future of your career, one pot might be labeled "success/raise/promotion," another labeled "layoff/failure," and the third labeled "no change—stagnation." The first plant to sprout indicates the strongest energies at this time.

The second approach was utilized to predict the weather. Three onions were cut in half and the resulting six halves placed in a row in the attic on New Year's Eve. They represented the next six months in succession from right to left. Come New Year's day those halves that are damp indicate a likewise rainy month (those that are dry— a dry month). In terms of applying this to our household efforts you might interpret the damp halves as months where there are tears, or where your life is "watered" by something or someone. Dry months could be regarded as uneventful, or perhaps a bit tight financially.

Tea

Tea was introduced to China around 500 C.E., and historians believe that the custom of tea reading started not long afterward. However, we don't have a lot of written records to go on. We know that Romans scried the remnants of fruit and pulp in the bottom of wine glasses, and we know that, after tea drinking was established in Europe in the 1700s, actual systems of tea reading became known. We also know that Gypsy traditions are likely to thank for its popularity on both continents.

Tasseography, tea leaf reading's formal name, owes its verbiage to the Middle English word *tasse*, which means cup. This art reached a height of popularity in the Victorian era, where tea leaf reading often accompanied noontime visits among friends and family. Personal taste often dictated the type of tea utilized for a reading. However, experienced readers commonly recommended a broad-leafed mix for clarity, and possibly chose the flavor or aroma so it reflected the question at hand.

At the start of a tea leaf reading, the querent holds the cup in his or her left hand. Then while thinking of a question, he or she swirls the tea in the cup clockwise thrice, taking at least one sip. Next, the cup gets placed upside down on a saucer and is allowed to drain for a moment.

Some readers will tap the bottom lightly before righting the cup to shake loose any excess leaves. Finally the emerging patters are read. Those nearest the edge of the cup relate to the present and near future; those in the center talk of things farther away in time or emotionally.

Here's a list of some of the shapes and their common interpretive values:

- **Acorn:** Victory or success that also provides foundations or security.
- **Ant:** Hard work and persistence pay off.
- **Arrow:** Bad news is coming your way, often in a letter.
- **Bat:** Beware—someone or something is not what it seems.
- **Banana:** Business dealings (sometimes a trip).
- **Bed:** Peace or contentment.
- **Bee:** Social activity.
- **Bell:** Announcement (sometimes a wedding).
- **Bird:** Messages—are you listening?
- **Branch:** A new companion or friend.
- **Bridge:** Overcoming; growth; development.
- **Butterfly:** Avoid vanity.
- **Cage:** Restrictions.
- **Candle:** Kindness from others.
- **Cat:** New beginnings; landing on your feet.
- **Circle:** Love or protection.
- **Clock:** Need to act in a timely manner.
- **Clumps:** Barriers and delays.
- **Cross:** Decisions.
- **Crown:** Honor; rewarded efforts.
- **Cup:** Give to receive.

- **Diamond:** An unexpected gift.
- **Dice:** Don't take a gamble.
- **Dog:** Faithful companions and good advice.
- **Door:** Opportunity awaits.
- **Drum:** Gossip.
- **Ear:** News coming your way—listen!
- **Egg:** A new project proves successful.
- **Eye:** Keep your eyes open—be cautious.
- **Fan:** Flirting with someone or some idea.
- **Fire:** Haste makes waste.
- **Flag:** Imminent danger.
- **Fork:** A dilemma.
- **Gate:** The solution is before you.
- **Glass:** Delicacy is needed here.
- **Glove:** A challenge (often personal).
- **Grape:** Joyous occasions.
- **Hammer:** Buildup of stress or anger.
- **Hat:** Try something new.
- **Horse:** Movement, especially in relationships.
- **House:** Foundations and security.
- **Ivy:** Loyal friends and family.
- **Jug:** Party or social activity.
- **Key:** Change—be ready to roll with it.
- **Kite:** Hopes or wishes fulfilled.
- **Knife:** An ending or separation.
- **Ladder:** Things are looking up; advancement.
- **Leaf:** Good luck.
- **Letters:** Alphabetical letters often reference a name.
- **Lock:** Something holding you back.
- **Moon:** Romance or love.

- **Mountain:** Difficulties.
- **Mouse:** Frugality; losses.
- **Nail:** An enemy.
- **Net:** Something unseen that trips you up.
- **Numbers:** Reference time frames (hours, days, weeks, months, years).
- **Owl:** Take care of your health; be true to self.
- **Pentagram:** Trust your reason and logic to guide you.
- **Pillar:** Achievements.
- **Pinecone**: Fertility or abundance.
- **Pipe:** The muse or creativity.
- **Purse:** Financial setback (only temporary).
- **Question mark:** Transformation or uncertainty.
- **Rainbow:** Unusually good fortune.
- **Rake:** The need for structure or order.
- **Ring:** Love and marriage.
- **Saw:** A stranger causes disruption.
- **Scales:** Measure your choice carefully.
- **Seal:** Don't overextend yourself—focus.
- **Ship:** An adventure or trip.
- **Snake:** An enemy in your midst.
- **Spear:** Bad news.
- **Spider:** Monetary improvement.
- **Staff:** Culpability.
- **Stairs:** Change in condition.
- **Star:** Fortune or fate.
- **Sun:** Blessings.
- **Sword:** Arguments.
- **Teapot:** Business gathering of some importance.
- **Tree:** A goal reached.

· **Turtle:** Criticism, not always merited.

· **Umbrella:** Worry—don't make this bigger than it really is.

· **Violin:** Hermitage.

· **Volcano:** Some type of eruption.

· **Watch:** Recuperation.

· **Waterfall:** Influence; abundance.

· **Web:** Complexity; red tape.

· **Wine glass:** Hospitality; new connections.

· **Wreath:** Extreme happiness.

SAMPLE READING

The question: Am I persuing the best course of action to achieve success in my artistic field?

The reading: Toward the rim are an ant and a bridge; toward the middle of the cup, a star, and at the bottom of the cup, a rake and a pipe. Overall this seems like a fairly positive reading. You can achieve success through hard work and overcome whatever obstacles you feel hinder you. However, you should be aware that the hand of fate plays a role here, and that you need to remain focused and organized in order for your muse to find full expression.

Chapter 14

Geomancy

Nature speaks in symbols and signs.
—John Greenleaf Whittier

Geomancy covers a wide variety of systems, from observation of the Earth's physical configurations to interpreting the patterns of dirt when scattered on the ground. We find systems of geomancy in places as diverse as Scandinavia, Africa, Arabia, and India. One of the simplest systems I found was written about in *Napoleon's Book of Fate*. It requires the querent create a line of random holes in the dirt with a stick while thinking of his or her question. This is repeated 16 times. Any line that has an *even* number of dots becomes two dots for interpretation, and any *odd* number becomes a single dot. The resulting patterns (four consecutive sets of four) may then be interpreted using the same values as those provided in Chapter 10 (pages 144-146).

For those of you who live in somewhat unpredictable or inclement environments, there are other media through which to utilize this system. For example, you could poke holes in mashed potatoes using a toothpick. The potatoes are certainly an "earthy" crop, and the toothpick is a miniature stick! Or, draw random dots on a piece of paper 16 times and add up the results.

As an aside, both of these adaptive options have potential on another level. If the reading you get from the mashed potatoes is very positive, you might want to consume them to internalize those energies. If the reading you get from the paper is likewise positive, you could carry it as part of a charm bag or amulet. And if the paper results seemed negative—how about burning that swatch as part of a banishing spell? Ultimately, the outcome of divinatory efforts depends heavily on what you do with the information, so I encourage you to think along these lines regularly.

SAMPLE READING

The question: The querent has been out of work due to another person's error or dishonesty. Coming home from what seemed to be a really good interview, he or she wants to get a feel for the potential outcome.

The reading: Let's say the original pattern looked like this:

The first row has six holes, and the second row has four, so both even numbers have a geomantic equivalent of 2. The third and forth rows have five and three holes, respectively, so both odd numbers translate to a single dot. Therefore, the resulting pattern would be as follows:

This pattern represents luck, blessings, and karmic balance. The reading would imply either that the job for which the querent just interviewed is very promising (or another opportunity is right around the corner), but also that somehow there will be a balance point for the person who put him or her in this mess to begin with.

Chapter 15

Random Systems

> *For better or worse, our future will be*
> *determined in large part by our dreams*
> *and by the struggle to make them real.*
> —Mihaly Csikszentmihalyi

Random divination systems base their interpretive values on something wholly unpredictable to the querent. One example comes to us from Greece. A person would go to Hermes' Shrine, whisper a question to the divine image, then plug his or her ears. Upon exiting the temple, the person would unblock their ears and trust that the first words they heard would be the god's answer. A similar system appeared in China in which a question would be posed to the Kitchen God late in January, and the first thing accidentally seen or overheard thereafter was accepted as the answer in literal or symbolic form.

As we review the various world cultures, we find many other examples of random systems, the inherent value being obvious—it's difficult to prejudice a system like this. You can't really preordain the results consciously or subconsciously. For example, meeting a clergy person on the way to a discussion is thought to be a very bad omen, accompanied with regrets. Nonetheless, it would be hard to predispose this meeting!

For our exploration, I want to first look at two more traditional random methods, then consider some potential modern adaptive methods, all of which you can do from the comfort of your own home.

Books

Divination with books is known as *bibliomancy*. The first mention of bibliomancy appears in Greece, where Homer's writing was used. That's why the practice of bibliomancy was sometimes referred to as *Homeretic lot casting* (and until the time when books were bound, it was also called *stichomancy*). In Rome, people preferred using Virgil's works, and in the Middle Ages, people turned to the Bible to try their hand at this oracular method.

The basic system of bibliomancy is wonderfully simple. Choose a book. Hold it in your hands while thinking of a question. With your eyes closed, open the book and place your index finger on a page. Whatever sentence your finger rests upon is the answer you seek.

Now, if you'd like to get fancier, Islamic tradition instructs that you pray before making an attempt, and then open the book three times. Note the seventh line of the left page each time, and compare them for your answer.

A third version of bibliomancy, properly called *rhapsodomancy*, uses random passages of poetry. In this case, if the sentence you land upon seems to make no sense, simply count the number of letters in it. An even number of letters is a positive omen.

If you wish, you can choose a book so that the theme matches that of your question (such as a romance novel for questions of love and relationships). Or you could create your own system out of Rolodex cards that utilizes all your favorite quotes. Pick out various lines from books or writers that you like. Copy them onto the cards. Once you're done, think of a question, spin the cards, and your answer appears before you when the spinning stops!

Spilling

In ancient Greek custom, wine became a favored substance for divination due to its association with Dionysus, who provided inspiration and foresight. In one particular method called *kottabos*, a cup of wine was tossed back and forth between people in a game-like manner. When the wine spilled, the results were interpreted similarly to an inkblot.

Other types of divination that utilized spilled liquids include ink (which portended petty annoyances) and milk (sadness). However, rather than *crying* over that spilled milk, they *scried* over it! And to my thinking, there's no reason why you couldn't utilize non-liquid items too, in the same way that spilled salt portends bad luck. For example, if you spill a little flour on a damp surface, you could review the results for patterns that could be meaningful. Better still, this is a lot less messy than waiting to clean up liquid spills. For potential interpretive values, refer to the listing for tea leaves on pages 169-172.

Breakage

Closely related to divination by spilling, random items breaking indicated specific things to our ancestors. Here's a list of some of the omens for your consideration the next time something breaks:

- ☙ Breaking two dishes in one day talks of rushing and lack of focus.
- ☙ Breaking two eggs is a good omen for love, but only one says to be careful all day.
- ☙ A needle breaking during sewing improves luck. If it breaks in the machine, expect news.

෧෨ Breaking a bottle brings minor misfortunes.

෧෨ Breaking green glass portends disappointments, while red glass predicts anxiety.

෧෨ Breaking one side of a pair of scissors warns of problems in the home.

෧෨ Breaking chopsticks is a bad omen especially for family financially stability.

While these are very generalized, if you had a specific question on your mind when the breakage happens, try looking for patterns in the remnants too.

Findings

Throughout Europe and early America, finding certain objects was thought to dictate particular fates depending on what question laid heavy on your mind. Here are some examples for your consideration when next you stumble over something unexpected:

· **Buttons or snippets of wire:** Good fortune.

· **Hairpin:** A new friendship.

· **Holey stones found by the water:** A gift of the sea that should be carried for blessings.

· **Horseshoe:** A positive omen, especially for luck.

· **Iron Nail:** An unexpected windfall.

· **Needles:** Company arriving.

· **Pin:** Poor luck when its head is facing away from you.

· **A square item:** The need to organize.

· **A triangular item:** Release fear and put your energy to better use.

· **A diamond-shaped item:** Protection; move ahead with confidence.

· **An item with an X on it:** Respect is the key to resolving your question.

If you like this system, consider adding more items to it, and give each a specific meaning. For example, finding a tack could portend a difficult road where caution is required, and a piece of jewelry could portend a forth-coming gift. Other ideas include a gum wrapper repre-senting the need to improve communications, a shoelace symbolizing something waiting to trip you up, and a battery counseling that you should watch your energy.

Another way to interpret your findings is by their color. This concept originated in the Seneca tradition, where the Elders teach that nature's gifts can provide important insights into life's nagging questions. Here's the correspondences they give:

- **Black:** Hear the truth; have strong faith and stronger convictions.
- **Blue:** Serve the truth; trust your instincts and be creative.
- **Brown:** Accept the truth; balance your ego and be wholly responsible.
- **Green:** Live the truth; be dependable and compassionate.
- **Grey:** Honor the truth; use your knowledge and develop your skills.
- **Orange:** Learn the truth; try to relate to all aspects of this situation; focus on kinship.
- **Pastels:** See the truth before you; find your potential; watch for prophetic dreams.
- **Pink:** Work for truth; give service to others and aid the All.
- **Purple:** Give thanks for the truth; strive for wholeness and healing.
- **White/Crystal:** Walk in truth; be ready to both give and receive.
- **Yellow:** Love the truth; use compassion.

A neat adaptation of this idea is to gather marbles, one of each color, and put them in a bag. When you have a nagging question, pull out one of the marbles and interpret it according to this color key, or one of your own devising. This way you can add more colors or color blends and increase potential interpretive values.

Insects

Traditionally, household superstitions have included animal signs (specifically those of pets). But what of insects? Yes, like so many other natural items, insect behavior was also observed and interpreted. Because most of these critters exist in a variety of environments and sometime show up in our homes, I'm including them in random divination. In other words, if you want to figure out what's really bugging you, check on this list!

· **Ants:** If there's an ants' nest near your door, providence is on its way.

· **Bees:** Bees swarming near a person or a home speaks of endings or death. Being stung by a bee represents a betrayal. Bees flying around you portend important messages, and dreaming of bees indicates you'll receive some type of honor soon. A bee landing on your lips and flying off symbolizes the gift of the Muse.

· **Beetle:** One walking over your shoe brings bad luck for that day.

· **Butterfly:** A butterfly that comes into the house tells of a wedding or another positive partnership.

· **Cricket:** Crickets in your home are an omen of good fortune and domestic bliss.

· **Grasshoppers:** When these appear near you, they bring good luck, especially in travels.

· **Katydid:** When you hear the first katydid of the season, it talks of either frost, or a similarly chilly disposition.

· **Ladybug:** Watch to see where the ladybug flies, to know in which direction your true love lies.

· **Lightning bug:** In late spring, a good fishing season or, more mundanely, prosperity.

· **Moth:** Success or the arrival of an important letter.

· **Praying mantis:** When one lands on your hand, you'll soon meet a distinguished person or gain some type of honor.

· **Wasp:** A warning to guard against jealousy or lies.

By the way, these harbingers need not show up in living form. They might appear as an image on a pack of matches you're given, a business card, the flyer for a local store, and so forth.

VCR or DVD

Now that we've looked at some of what the ancients were doing, let's consider the wonders of technology and the alternatives they offer us. Now I know that some people might consider the idea of using a VCR or DVD player for random divination a bit odd, but stop and reconsider. Didn't our ancestors use everything that had meaning to them for oracular efforts? Didn't they adapt and add new things as various items came into popular usage? Why not follow that example?

Our VCRs and DVD players "record" information in two formats, then play that information back to us. So instead of choosing a book with an appropriate theme, how about a video tape or disk with a theme that pertains to your question? Now instead of holding the book, you'll keep your finger on the fast forward feature of the machine while thinking of a question. Close your eyes and focus, lifting your finger when you feel so inclined. Now, watch and listen for the next minute or so (take notes or rewind and watch again until you have the information). Review this with regard to your question, looking for:

- Key words or phrases: For example, if you were thinking about a trip, and the segment of the tape or disk mentions danger or delays, you may want to reconsider. Similarly, character names may hold import. If you were wondering about your happiness and the main character's name is Joy, that could be your omen.

- Color cues: Is there a predominant color for this scene? If so, how does that relate to your question? If you were thinking about love, for example, and the predominant color was blue, I'd wonder if you're sad, or if you're feeling peaceful.

- Settings: Where does this scene take place? If your question centered around work, and the scene is an office place, it's a strong indicator that you've gotten the right piece of information and just need to interpret it.

- Art or other items in the scene that could have symbolic value: If you've been contemplating studying plant spirits and learning how to work with them, and the predominant wallpaper or decorative touches in the scene are flowers, that's a positive sign.

Because the visual arts can be filled to overflowing with potential symbols, I suggest looking at the scene as a whole first, then breaking down the component parts if a meaning isn't immediately obvious, much as you might break down dream symbolism.

By the way, if you don't have a video or DVD, a radio or tape player can function perfectly well. With the radio, keep it turned off while you're thinking of a question and adjusting the station knob. Turn it on and tune until you hear something clearly (I really like the symbolic value here of "tuning in" to what you most need to hear). For the tape player, just push fast forward until you feel ready to release the button and listen.

Surfing Sorcery

Another item that's come into our lives with a flourish is the computer. It's nearly impossible to go to work, turn on a TV, or drive down the highway without hearing or seeing something about bytes, RAM, drives, and modems. As an ardent techno-Pagan, I got to thinking about how this item has become a symbol, and how that symbolism might be used in our magick (in this case, divinatory efforts).

As any time I ponder such things, my first question is: *For what do I use this item?* The words I correlate with computers are information retrieval (very apt for divination), communication (also suitable), and record-keeping. Looking to information retrieval first, most folks use a search engine to find what they want on the Internet. So, taking that one step further, why not use that same search engine in a type of random divination effort?

To try this yourself go to your favorite engine. Relax and take a deep breath while thinking of a question. Boil that question down into several words or phrases. Type those into the search engine and hit enter. Look over the listings that come up and click on one randomly. If that takes you to another link you can either read what first comes to your attention, or go on to the next page. Let your instincts guide you.

> ## SAMPLE READING
>
> *The question:* During the writing of this book, the publisher hoped I might finish early for a variety of reasons, so I wondered what divine insight might reveal.
>
> *The reading:* I did an Internet search for "finish, book, early." The first link I chose took me to a site with this phrase across the top banner: "Become a member of Enchanted Learning." That in itself seemed to be a very positive omen that finishing the book early would help it somehow. The second link took me to the phrase "starting out right"—again, a secondary confirmation. You get the idea. Give it a try.

Chapter 16

Scrying

> *A human being is only interesting if he's in contact with himself. I learned you have to trust yourself, be what you are, and do what you ought to do the way you should do it. You have got to discover you, what you do, and trust it.*
>
> —Barbra Streisand

The term *scrying* comes from *descry*, meaning "to discover." The basic description for this method is that of looking upon a surface in search of prophetic patterns. While crystal scrying is the most widely known version of this technique, many other mediums were used including ink, water, blood, fire, and cloud patterns. Many of the instructions accompanying these systems suggested some type of cleansing and purification beforehand, such as bathing, fasting, or prayer. Let's begin by looking at *crystallomancy*.

Crystals

Unlike the rather stereotypic images of a person staring into a crystal sphere, crystallomancy also utilized polished cross sections of glass or stone (also properly called *lithomancy* in the Western world, and *Me-lon* in Tibet—the only difference being that the Tibetan system adds recited mantras to the mix). St. Augustus felt that crystallomancy originated in Persia, where beryl spheres were the preferred media. Historical treatises indicate that this art was also popular among Romans, who introduced it into Europe.

By the fifth century c.e., texts reveal various types of crystals being favored in Europe, including aquamarine, quartz, and obsidian. In Ireland, beryl was mentioned. By the 1300s, crystallomancy was used regularly to discover thieves and recover their booty. Come the 1400s, Swiss alchemist Paracelsus described scrying as "observing rightly" and understanding what one sees.

It was around the same time that Mages developed rituals to ensure successful scrying efforts. Besides the purifying efforts, other recommendations included reciting invocations, placing the crystal in an ornate stand with sigils, and anointing the crystal with olive oil. All this effort was aimed at awakening the crystal's indwelling spirit, who would then respond with imagery. Similarly, the Cherokee divining crystals were sometimes "fed" deer's blood to keep the spirit of the stone both vital and appeased.

In the Yucatán, the crystal scryer was known as a *b'men*. These people used clear stones for divinatory efforts, especially lost items. The Shamans recommended that a scryer sleep with his or her crystal to improve sympathy between the user and the tool. They also suggested rubbing the crystal with mugwart, passing it through copal incense, and dipping it in rum prior to use. Beyond this, the diviner himself or herself would drink a cup of chicory tea to prepare for the rite. Any or all of these ideas can be added to your personal scrying efforts.

As a general rule of thumb, a crystal or glass of about 3 inches across is comfortable for the human eye. This is also a large enough surface to allow for clear images. Some people prefer a clear, faceted surfaces, such as Austrian crystal. Others like a natural crystal that has some type of inclusions on which the eye can catch. If you're a novice scryer, I think you will find that stones with clouds or inclusions produce results more quickly than absolutely clear ones.

Place the crystal against a dark surface, like black or blue velvet. Dim your lights a bit, and (if you wish) have a candle burning nearby. Sit quietly, maintain your focus and purpose, and take a deep breath. Look toward the crystal, or at a point just behind it. Don't worry about blinking—just relax and let your vision blur a bit. You're watching for clouds to form and swirl. Be patient. This often takes a bit of practice to get the hang of it.

Here's a list of some of the traditional interpretive values:

- **Ascending clouds:** A positive outcome or "yes" answer.
- **Black clouds:** A negative omen.
- **Blue clouds staying level near the center:** Balance and peace.
- **Blue, violet, or green clouds:** Joy; good news.
- **Brown clouds:** Matters of practicality.
- **Descending clouds:** A negative outcome or "no" answer.
- **Green clouds moving up or right:** Financial improvements.
- **Orange clouds:** Community or social situations.

- **Pink clouds moving upward:** Friendship; health improvements.
- **Purple clouds:** Matters of spirit.
- **Red clouds:** Strong emotions, sometimes anger or passion.
- **White clouds:** A positive omen.
- **Yellow clouds moving downward:** Betrayal.
- **Yellow or red clouds:** Danger or trouble lurking nearby—go slowly.

As an aside, some people see symbols or images instead of clouds, and some people loose sight of the crystal altogether and the pictures take on lifelike proportions. That's wonderful; but it's relatively rare. Try not to focus on the image so closely that the intuitive process stops (thinking about the image engages your logical, conscious mind). Let the symbols or pictures flow until they naturally seem to stop, then write up your experience. You can compare the imagery to that of dream interpretation guides.

When your crystal isn't in use, keep it wrapped in a soft, natural cloth, someplace safe. Periodically charge the stone by leaving it in the light of the full moon so it's filled with intuitive energy.

Mirrors

A Swiss alchemist by the name of Paracelsus put forth a recommended process for making magick mirrors. It was very time-consuming and included the melting of expensive metals, precisely measured, at an auspicious astrological time. The whole thing took weeks, after which the mirror was polished for use. The ritualistic overtones in Paracelsus's method were impossible to overlook, and they speak heavily of the influence of both folklore and superstition in our ancestors' thinking.

Paracelsus wasn't alone in his ideas or elaborate processes. European Mages invoked a spirit to live in their mirrors and answer questions. This made the mirror a kind of living thing, but it's not necessarily a process I recommend. And while you could consider creating an Elemental for this purpose (an Elemental is an empowered entity with a limited life span that's based in the power of Earth, Air, Fire, or Water), I think the Kitchen Witch's motto of KISS (keep it simple and sublime) applies here.

One thing is certain, magick mirrors bridge the gap between this world and the astral. They open a window into both space and time for the user and can even be used for communication over long distances, like a telephone line. Consequently, like a Ouija board, it might be best to use this tool in a sacred space so that any unwanted energies or spirits are neatly kept at bay.

Before going into the process of making your own mirror, you should know that the ancients often used other items for scrying. Anything with a polished or reflective surface will do the trick. So you probably have a few items at home that could become a make-shift magick mirror when you're pressed for time—such as the back of a soup spoon!

Making a Magick Mirror

1. Get a picture frame that's got a glass surface. Any size or shape is fine. I have one small pocket-sized frame in pewter, and another bathroom sized frame in wood. You may, however, find that a darker frame helps the process of scrying. If you're on a budget, I've often had good luck getting frames at dollar stores and even second hand shops for less than $5.

2. If you want to decorate the frame in any way,
    now's the time to do it. I have a friend who
    carved runes into the border of his, and another
    person I know painted personal symbols onto
    the wood.

3. Purchase a can of black enamel spray paint—
    high gloss (typically available at hardware
    stores and craft shops). Dark green or dark
    purple will work too. Make sure the paint will
    take to glass surfaces.

4. Clean off the glass surface making sure there's
    no lint or fingerprints on either side. If you
    wish, this is also a good time to spiritually
    cleanse the glass as well. I recommend using
    a little lemon water so you can accomplish
    both things at the same time!

5. Put down a protective surface on which you
    can paint the glass. I recommend cardboard
    or newspaper. Place the glass carefully on
    that surface (don't get fingerprints on it!).
    Proper ventilation is necessary, but I do not
    recommend working where it's windy, as that
    can blow dirt into the paint or cause running.

6. At this juncture, you can consider adding a
    liquid condenser to the project. The idea be-
    hind this condenser is that it improves the
    overall magnetic energy in your finished tool.
    I prefer a tincture of mugwort, sage, willow,
    orange, and sandalwood. Other potential in-
    gredients are any lunar herbs, spider webs,
    salt, rosewater, cinnamon, bay, lily, jasmine
    and marigold. Sprinkle your blend over the
    surface of the mirror and let it dry com-
    pletely before painting (note that mirrors
    with condensers may need an extra layer of
    paint to achieve a smooth surface).

7. Spray an even layer of paint on the entire glass. Let this dry completely then add a second and third coat (note that the paint MUST dry in between each coat so the surface doesn't get lumpy)

8. If you want to add some fine opalescent glitter to your mirror, spray the front with a coat of clear finish and sprinkle the glitter on the wet surface. Many students find that the glitter gives their eyes something to "catch" on so they experience more success with scrying from the get-go. The effect is also very visually appealing, looking like stars in a night sky. If you want, you can add another clear coat so the glitter will not flake off.

9. Once the last coat has dried, put the glass back into the frame, glass side out (again watch your fingerprints).

10. Cover the mirror with a lint free, natural cloth for storage.

Last but not least, before using the mirror you should bless and charge it. And like so many other things, the process for this often varied with the person you consulted for ideas. A 16th-century procedure instructed burying the mirror in a grave for three weeks (YUCK!). Once dug up, the spirit in the mirror was to be awakened on a Tuesday at 1 a.m., 8 a.m., or 10 p.m.—all hours associated with Mars.

Thankfully there's another idea from the same time period that's much more functional. In this case we'll anoint the mirror with a special oil. To prepare the oil, you'll need a teaspoon each of thyme, cinnamon, chamomile, and rosemary, all of which support psychic endeavors. Put these in a pan with 1/4 cup of good quality olive oil. Simmer until the blend smells like a strong herbal tea. Cool this and dab it on the mirror's frame moving clockwise as you go. If you wish now's a good time to say a prayer or add an incantation to further empower your tool.

Store the remaining oil in a dark, airtight bottle. You can use this on your third eye and pulse points anytime in the future just before a scrying effort. It acts as both a blessing and subtle aromatherapy.

If you'd like other options for blessing your mirror, how about breathing on it and saying a prayer? Breath equates to life and spirit in nearly every culture. Better still, this helps align the mirror with your personal vibrations.

When you're done blessing the mirror, cover it again and put it away until the next waxing moon cycle. The mirror needs a little time to "settle" from the creation process. Using it during the waxing to full moon also emphasizes the intuitive nature more. After that time, start working with your mirror regularly. The more you practice with it, the more the mirror will respond positively. Here's how:

1. Make sure you're well rested and in a good state of mind before trying to scry. Negativity will often create similarly negative imagery.

2. Clear the mirror using a little bit of witch hazel tincture (you can buy this at most drug stores). This will eliminate any unwanted energy that the mirror may have picked up between uses.

3. Take the mirror to an area where you won't be interrupted, and one that's fairly neutral in terms of your personal feelings. Some areas of our homes have bad memories associated with them, and those memories will not help your divinatory efforts.

4. Put the mirror on a surface where it will be at eye level when you sit across from it. Keep the mirror at what you consider a comfortable reading distance from yourself.

5. Get comfortable. Make sure there's nothing around that might distract you.

6. Take three deep, cleansing breaths and relax. If it helps, close your eyes for a few minutes so you can center and focus.

7. Take time to "tune in" to your mirror. This tool, like anything you've created, has a unique vibrational frequency that you need to come to know on an intimate level. Feel how it tingles on the edge of your auric awareness. Say a gentle "hello" to that energy, then reach out and lift up the cloth covering.

8. As in crystal gazing, it seems to be easiest to look at a point just beyond the mirror while you allow your eyes to unfocus.

9. Express your question out loud or in your mind. Be clear and concise.

10. If this is among your first scrying efforts, don't try to go for hours at a time. About 10 minutes a day, to begin, is about right. You can slowly increase the time as you become more proficient. Remember you have to retrain your mind to deal with this *one* issue, rather than the many on which you're normally focused. Also, you're presently disengaging the conscious self so that the higher self can "see." This also takes practice, and trying to do too much too soon often causes both eye strain and headaches. Most people find that within 6 weeks they can handle 20 minute sessions. Nonetheless,

when your body says stop, please listen. You'll have no positive results after that point anyway.

11. Pay attention to all your senses—not just the visual input. Some people find that rather than "seeing" things in the mirror this tool opens other sensual cues. They end up smelling, tasting, or hearing something instead! Note, there's nothing wrong with this. It's just another way our mind interprets extra-sensory information on a concrete level. These experiences are just as valid, and have just as much potential interpretive value as visual input. For example, if you were thinking about a particular situation and suddenly the room seemed to fill with a pleasant aroma of flowers—that would be a positive sign of a good scenario for you.

12. If images start to appear, try not to "hold" them; rather let it flow like a movie. You can make note of what you saw right after you're done so that everything's fresh and clear.

13. When input ceases to come forward or you've reached your physical time limit, put the cloth back over your mirror and make your notes.

Now, the next obvious question is how to go about interpreting what you see when images begin to come. Most people feel that mirror scrying works on two levels, the first being personal experience and the second being universal archetypes (akin to dream interpretation). Your first impressions of what an image or symbol means are of ultimate importance to interpreting what you've seen. There's a lot of subjectivity here that a book of interpretive values cannot provide.

The most common vision people experience is that of moving clouds or bits of light that dance or float. These may be interpreted as follows:

- ☙ The darker the image the larger the warning.
- ☙ The brighter the image, the better the omen.
- ☙ Darkness broken up by light means reason for hope (an improvement).
- ☙ Movement up or right is a "yes" answer.
- ☙ Movement down or left is a "no" answer.
- ☙ Circling light or clouds indicate that fate is too convoluted right now for any specific answer to be given.
- ☙ Concentric circles represent the need to narrow your focus and prioritize.
- ☙ Bright red clouds counsel the need to balance your emotions.
- ☙ Yellow clouds imply that communication problems lie at the heart of your question (especially if moving down or to the left).
- ☙ Orange light or clouds talk of using your skills to reap rewards.
- ☙ Green clouds speak of financial opportunities or personal growth.
- ☙ Blue clouds moving up speak of joy and contentment.
- ☙ Purple clouds deal with spiritual matters or things very personal to you.
- ☙ Pink clouds represent close friends and partnerships.

Again, note both the direction of movement and the color for more insights. As time goes on you'll probably start to see actual images and pictures, but usually that requires several months of practice. When this does happen, pay attention to the order in which images appear, where they are on the mirror's surface, and how far away they seem from you in terms of distance. The order of the images often imply a time line, or what things are most important. The distance also can speak of time (namely how far in the future you're seeing).

If a symbol appears and reappears in your work—pay attention! Just as with dream work, your superconscious is trying to tell you something important. If you'd like a more complete exploration of magick mirrors, try reading my *Little Book of Mirror Magick* (The Crossing Press).

Computer and TV Screens

Now that we've covered good methods for scrying using traditional items, it's time to turn to technology. The modern world has given us two terrific media for scrying that are right under our noses. Nonetheless, the first time I tell people about the idea of using a TV or computer screen for divination efforts they typically respond by laughing or staring at me incredulously. If you're agreeing with them, stop and ask yourself one question. What do you expect to happen when you turn on the TV or computer screen? You expect pictures to appear! What better psychological edge could we give ourselves than to have a preconditioned positive expectation?

To utilize either one of these, I do suggest turning the item on (again it's the expectation that's helpful here, and we don't expect images from a turned-off system). For the TV, set it to an input station so you still have a black screen with power to it. For the computer, you can create a black screen saver for yourself, or open a blank page with a program that allows you to and change the background color to black, dark purple, or dark blue. Return to the instructions for scrying with a crystal and follow accordingly!

Chapter 17

Helpful Hints

*The future belongs to those who believe in
the beauty of their dreams.*

—Eleanor Roosevelt

Symbols and Pictographs

Symbols are very important to your new divinatory
abilities. They represent the shapes of power, cosmic
law, and universal truths for which words seem to be
wanting. An experienced diviner learns to identify these
emblems even if only partially formed, and interpret
them accordingly. Nonetheless, the sheer volume of symbols that could appear seems daunting to even the most
experienced practitioner. Because of this, I strongly recommend buying a book or two that has pictographs and
symbols with their varying cultural meanings. There are
three to which I regularly refer that you can often find
in good, used condition at *www.amazon.com*:

∾ *The Illustrated Book of Signs and Symbols*,
     Miranda Bruce-Mitford (DK Publishing,
     1996). Full color illustrations.

∾ *Illustrated Encyclopaedia of Traditional
     Symbols*, J.C. Cooper (Thames & Hudson,
     1978).

∾ *The Woman's Dictionary of Symbols and
     Sacred Objects*, Barbara Walker (Harper &
     Row, 1988).

I believe you'd find any of these three an invaluable helpmate to your kitchen divination efforts.

Furthering Divination Efforts

While we might wish otherwise, divination isn't something that always comes easily to everyone. People struggle with their humanness, with the sense that those inner nudges are nothing more than indigestion or weird quirks. If you find yourself in those shoes, don't despair; you're not alone, you're not the first, and there are things that can help you get past those natural insecurities. The first is considering making yourself a divination altar.

An altar, by its nature, symbolizes the Divine interacting in our lives (as a natural part of it—the key here being *natural*. You want to begin stressing psychism as something that's perfectly normal and your spiritual nature as a part of every moment of every day). For those who plan to petition a god or goddess for assistance in divinatory efforts, setting up your altar in a special manner makes especially good sense. For one, you can leave your chosen tool there for a while before a reading to absorb sacred energies. For another, creating an altar focuses your mind and spirit on your goal, and improves the overall vibrations with which you're working.

The divination altar can be as complex or simple as you wish. Begin by finding a flat surface that won't be disturbed once you're done. I use both the top of my television console or the top of my bookshelf where both pets and children cannot reach. Then find a natural cloth covering. Use a color that either symbolizes your question, or one that highlights the type of system you've chosen. For example, dark cloths help with crystal scrying. I prefer a plain white cloth for stone castings, or a yellow cloth to highlight the Air element, which rules divination.

Next, add your chosen tool, candles, and perhaps some empowering incense. Aromatics trusted for improving psychic insights include anise, lilac, and sandalwood. Also consider having some type of representation of the deity on whom you plan to call present in the center of that space. A statue, a lit white candle, or any items sacred to that being are all good choices.

You can leave your altar up for a long time, or only have it present for your reading. I like setting mine up at least a few hours before using my tools to help set the tone in my workspace. I also often use the altar's surface itself for laying out or casting the reading. As long as you have enough space, you might want to try that approach and see if it improves your results, because this is a small sacred space that should support your goals.

When you do take down your altar, I recommend storing all the things you've gathered in one place, and preferably one that's somehow special. Leave a little note inside as to the purpose for these tools (in case you don't use them a lot, you won't forget their function this way). Keeping things together like this creates sympathy between each component that will help empower your next divinatory effort.

Speaking of storage, another thing I have found somewhat helpful is creating a special housing for my divination tools. I've made hand-sewn pouches, decorated wooden boxes, and lined dresser drawers to devise a safe, nest-like haven in which my tools can reside. To that foundation I often add protective herbs or aromatics such as white sage.

You might be asking how this would help divination efforts. The answer is twofold. First, it keeps the items away from stray energies that could skew a reading. Secondly, as you're preparing that space for your tools, you're thinking about them—about what they mean to you, and about their place in your magickal life. That thought process is like a meditation that improves the rapport between you and your implements, which, in turn, provides you with more accurate results when you use them!

We've talked a bit already about calling on various powers for assistance in your art. When you come to the end of yourself and seem unable to find any assistance in your tools, this would seem a logical next step. In the appendix, I've provided a list of gods and goddesses who are known for helping with various forms of divination. Look this over and see if there's a being to whom you relate, and one with whom you're willing to build a relationship. One does not simply walk up to a stranger's door and start asking for help. Similarly, one does not simply begin entreating an unknown power for assistance. But if you take the time to get to know a persona, and find suitable ways of honoring that being in your sacred space, working with Deity in divination can prove very beneficial (or minimally help you overcome some of those bumps you've experienced).

Keep diligent notes on the divination systems you've tried and your experiences with each. This notebook serves several functions. First, you can return to it when you've decided that you need to try a new system. Here you can quickly scan various trials and determine which were the most successful. Second, you can also review the readings you've done for yourself and see if there are any new perspectives to be found therein.

Finally, don't give up trying. Each person has an inner psychic just waiting to get out. It's just that we've been taught for so long to think and live logically that it takes time to retrain our mind and spirit and allow those gifts space in our reality. Be as patient with yourself as you would be with a child learning to walk, because for many of us, learning divination is that big of a step! I truly believe that with time and tenacity, you'll not only find a divinatory system that's perfect for you, but learn how to use it very successfully.

Gods and Goddesses of Divination

Chance is but the pseudonym of god for those particular cases which he does not chose to subscribe openly with his own sign-manual.

—S.T. Coleridge

It was not uncommon for the Priest, Priestess, Shaman, or Wise Person to consult the Divine before, during, or after a divinatory effort. After all, any being so great and powerful certainly would be able to help sort out elusive symbols and omens! Mind you, not all divine beings were credited with having predictive abilities, and not all had dominion over divinatory practices. Thus, this appendix provides an abbreviated overview of some of the beings directly associated with this ancient art.

If you choose to utilize this information on a personal level, I strongly advise getting to know a god or goddess more personally first. You need to understand the cultural context of the deity, know how to pronounce his or her name correctly, discover what items are suitable to honor that being in your sacred space, and of course approach that persona with suitable respect. Just as one would not randomly ask a total stranger for help with scrying or the tarot, developing a relationship with Deity is going to improve the results obtained by your request.

Akuj	African	Supreme god who governs the divinatory arts.
Apollo	Greek and Roman	God of prophesy who oversaw the Oracle at Delphi.
Artemis	Greek	Goddess who rules over psychic ability.
Brigit	Celtic	Goddess of inspiration and metaphysically obtained knowledge, especially pyromancy.
Carmenta	Roman	Goddess of prophesy. Festival dates 1/11 and 1/15.
Chang Kuo	Chinese	A patroness of the arts who used bamboo rods to evoke the souls of the dead for communicating oracular information. Call on her if using bamboo as a medium.
Daughter of Voice	Hebrew	A prophetic goddess who provided clues to a problem's solution via random divination (namely the first word or phrase overheard after invoking Her).
Demeter	Greek	Mistress of magick who is called upon for divination involving seeds, grain, or soil. Also suitable for consulting on questions of love.
Dione	Greek	Homer calls her the mother of Aphrodite. This goddess was the patroness of Dodona, and is appropriate for efforts that utilize trees, lots, and channeling.
Ea	Mesopo-tamian	God of oracles and fortune telling by Water.
Egeria	Roman	Another oracular goddess whose main Element was Water.
Fa	Benin	God of destiny. Fa knows each soul's fate.
Faunus	Roman	God of soothsaying.
Fortuna	Roman	Goddess of fate and fortune, often depicted as a wheel.

Freyja	Norse	Goddess of foresight, best called upon when using cats, Water, the moon, or flowers as focals or media.
Gabriel	Biblical	Angel of revelation and truth who presides over clairvoyance and Water scrying.
Gaia	Greek	The Oracle at Delphi originally belonged to Gaia before Apollo gained popularity. Gaia as a prophetess was invoked with oaths and offerings of fruit and grain.
Graiae	Greek	The Mothers of Greece, these spirits have all-seeing eyes, and as such, are great helpmates to scrying.
Hecate	Greek	The patroness of prophesy, especially those techniques that use the moon or a key.
Ida	Italian	The vital force of the heart, who presides over divinatory matters.
Ishtar	Assyrian and Babylonian	A divinatory goddess who personified Venus. As such, she was often consulted in matters of love and romance.
Isis	Egyptian	Goddess of good advice and divination, especially methods utilizing knots, string, or woven items.
Janus	Roman	The gatekeeper of beginnings and endings. This god has two faces, one of which looks to the future.
Katunda	E. African	God of oracles.
Kuan Ti	Chinese	God of fortune telling. Honor him with red and green candles (perhaps use these for your divination efforts).
Kusor	Phoenician	God of magick formulas and divination.
Massaya	Nicaraguan	Oracular goddess of volcanoes, invoke her when divining by Fire.
Mati Syra Zemlya	Slavonic	Goddess of divination, especially geomancy.
Merlin	British	Great Druid and prophet. Best called upon when utilizing crystals.

Michael	Biblical	Prince of wisdom and angel of divination, especially pyromancy.
Mithra	Persian	Sun god who presides over clairvoyance and prediction, especially anything involving Fire or sunlight.
Nerus	Greek	God of the sea and water credited with creating the divinatory art of hydromancy.
Nina	Chaldean	Goddess of oracles, especially those utilizing Water.
Norns	Teutonic	The three fates who weave the tapestry of a person's life. For prophetic insight Skold was the Norn of the future.
Odin	Norse	Chief god who created divinatory arts, specifically runes.
Orunmila	African	Yoruban prophet whose spirit is consulted for Ifa (divination that utilizes nuts, among other things).
Pan	Greek	God of soothsaying and natural omens.
Sakuna-devatas	Hindu	Goddess of all good omens.
Selene	Greek	Full-moon Goddess presiding over all lunar divinations.
Shair	Egyptian	God of destiny.
Shamash	Sumerian and Babylonian	God of divination, especially any utilizing the sun or rods.
Shaktis	Tibetan	An aspect of the supreme force who is called upon for clairvoyance and divination.
Shamash	Assyrian and Babylonian	An all-seeing sun god upon whom local seers called to reveal the future. Offerings of Water should precede asking for help with celestial signs and portents.
Siduri	Sumerian	Oracular goddess who gave prophets their words. Her offering is beer.
Svantovit	Slavonic	God of plenty, war, and prosperity. He has four heads that see in all directions to grant perspective.

Tezcat-lipuco	Mexican	God frequently called upon for visions especially those utilizing a mirror.
Themis	Greek	Greek goddess of good advice and oracles. Her festival is 2/28.
Thoth	Egyptian	God of divination and prophesy, especially numerology.
Tlazolteol	Aztec	Goddess of magick and divination, especially geomancy. Corn is a suitable offering for her.
Viracocha	Incan	God of oracles, especially Water-related ones.
Zaqar	Assyrian and Babylonian	God who brings prophetic dreams.
Zervan Akarana	Persian	God of time and destiny.
Zeus	Greek	The oracular center at Dodona was dedicated to him, as were the sacred oats that were observed for omens and signs there.

Index

A

aleuromancy, 164

alphitomancy, 158

altar, 200-201

Amazon.com, 55, 199

Artemidorus, 148

B

bartering for readings, 31-32

bibliomancy, 178

blessing tools, 65

books, divination with, 178-179
    history of, 178
    Islamic method of, 178

botanomancy, 109

C

candlemaking
    instructions for, 92-94
    Websites about, 92

candles
    divination with, 91-97
    interpreting flame of, 94-95
        interpreting wax of, 96-97

cards, divination with, 99-113
    history of, 99-100
    using coupons for, 106-108
    using greeting cards for,
        104-106
    using playing cards for,
        100-104

cards, tarot, 17, 20-22, 53-55, 57,
    59, 62-63, 99-100, 104-106,
    112, 143

cartomancy, 19, 99-113

cast systems, 115-127
    dice as, 120-123
    runes as, 123-126
    stones as, 116-119
    various objects used for,
        115-116, 126-127

casting cloth, values, 118

ceromancy, 91

channeling, 22

chants, 40
    Vedic, 41

charging, 66-68

clairvoyance, 42- 43
    cleansing as preparation
        for, 42

cleromancy, 120, 140

coins, 129-130
    history of, 129
    chart for reading, 130

colors, interpreting findings
    by, 181

components of psychic
    sensitivity, 43

crystallomancy, 187

crystals, 188-190
    history of, 188
    recommended size, 188
    interpretive values, 189-190

D

dactylomancy, 134

decoupage instructions, 82-83

dedication of tools, 65

developing your inner psychic,
    33-51

divination methods
    beans, 161-162
    board systems, 77-90
    books, 178-179
    bread, 158
    breakage, 179-180
    candle flame, 94-95
    canister top, 78-80
    cards, 99-113
    casting cloth, 118

cheese, 162

coffee creamer, 160

coffee grounds, 158-160
    list of patterns for, 159-160

coins, 129-130

computer screen, 198

corn, 162-163

coupons, 106-108
    interpretive values of, 107

crystals, 188-190

culinary theme, 84

dice, 120-123
    interpretive values of,
        120-122

dominoes, 140-141
    interpretive values of,
        140-141

dowsing, 131-137

drawn systems, 139-146

DVD, 183-185
    interpreting scenes, 184

eggs, 164

findings, by color, 191

flour, 164-165

flowers and plants, 109-113,
    142-143
    interpretive values of,
        110, 142-143

food findings, 157-172

fortune tablets, 86-90

geomancy, 173-174

greeting cards, 104-106

household omens and signs,
    153-156

insects, 182-183
    interpretive values of,
        182-183

Internet, 185-186

Kin, 77

mirrors, 190-198

Monopoly, 108-109

oil, 166-167
pendulums, 53-54, 134-137
    interpretive values of, 136
playing cards, 100-104
    interpretive values of,
        101-103
poetry, 178
random systems, 177-186
rods
    dowsing with, 131-133
    casting with, 143-146
runes, 123-126
    alternative symbols for, 124
    interpretive values of, 125
spilling, 179
stones, 116-119
symbol board, 81
tarot, 17, 20-22, 53-55, 57, 59,
    62-63, 99-100, 104-106,
    112, 143
tea leaves, 168-172
    interpretive values of,
        169-172
television screen, 198
VCR, 183-85
    interpreting scenes, 184
wax, 96-97

divination systems, 20
    adapting, 20, 57-58
    adding new symbols to, 58
    limitations of, 20
    making your own, 48-65
    storing and maintaining, 67-68

divination tools, 18
    cleansing of, 21
    charging of, 66
        Elemental method, 66-68
        with sun and moon, 66
        with visualization, 66
    protection of, 21
    storing, 202

divination,
    an altar and, 200-201
    ambience and, 49-50
    basics of, 15-32
    choosing a method that's
        right for you, 17
    common questions about, 16-32
    ethical, 30
    home systems of, 15
    Latin translation of, 22-23
    optimum times for, 48
    spiritual benefits of, 16-17
    steps for choosing a method
        of, 53-73
    types of, 17-19
    unusual media and, 35-36

dowsing, divination by, 131-137
    history of, 131
    rods for, 53, 132-133

drawn systems, divination and,
    139-146

dream
    aids, 147-153
        history of, 147-148
    catcher, 149-150
        blessing, 150
        easy-to-make version, 150
    sachet, 149
        how to create, 149
        dream-inducing foods, 151

dreams, prophetic, 147

E

Elementals, 191

Elements,
    card reading and, 63
    charging tools and, 66-68
    interpretive values of, 80

Exploring Candle Magick, 92

F

findings, divination with, 180-182
  examples and meanings
      of, 180
  interpretations by color, 181
florimancy, 109, 142
flowers, 109-113
  instructions for pressing,
      111-112
  interpretive values of, 142-143
  tarot spreads and, 112
  Victorian language of, 109-111
fortune cookies, making, 165-166
fortune tablets, 86-90
fortune-telling methods, 18

G

geomancy, divination by, 173-174
  history of, 173
  variations of, 174
God and divining, 24
gods and goddesses, divination
    and, 202
  list of, 205-209

H

handling the information you
    receive, 26
history of psychism, 34-36
home divination systems, 15
Homeretic lot casting, 178
household omens and signs,
    153-156
  list of folklore omens, 154-156

I

I Ching, 18, 116
  yarrow and, 18
*Illustrated Book of Signs and
    Symbols, The*, 200
*Illustrated Enciclodaedia of
    Traditional Symbols*, 200
incantations,
  for blessing candles, 93
  for empowering dream
      catcher, 44
  for focusing power of
      pendulum, 44-45
inner psychic, finding your, 36
invocations,
  candle-lighting, 44
  protecting sacred space
      and, 46
  thanking Powers and, 47

K

keeping your question a
    secret, 24
Kin divination system, 77
kottabos, 179

L

Language of Flowers, 110
lapandomancy, 91
lecanomancy, 166
lithomancy, 188
Little Book of Mirror Magick, 198
lychnomancy, 91

M

magickal potential, 33

making your own divination system, 58-65
  media for creating cards and, 60
  recording your values and, 64
  steps for, 59

mantras, 41
  personal, 41

meditation and visualization, 38

mediumship, 22

mirrors, 190-198
  blessing, 193-194
  interpreting images in, 196-197
  making a magick, 191-193
  preparing for a reading and, 194-196

O

omens and signs, 153-156

Oneirocritica, 148

oomantia, 163

Oracle at Delphi, 22

Ouija, 20, 77-78, 191

ovoscopy, 163

P

pendulums, 53-54, 134-137
  applications of, 134
  history of, 134
  interpretive values of, 136
  types of, 134-135

pessomancy, 116

pictographs, symbols and, 199-200

Posidonius, 34

prayer, 40

psychical research, 36

psychism, history of, 34-36

pyromancy, 91

pyroscopy, 91

R

reader,
  seeking a qualified, 17
  signs of a questionable, 25
  signs of an ethical, 30

reading
  for a group, 71-72, 96
  for others, 70-71
  for yourself, 32, 68-70

readings,
  extra cards or stones pulled at the end of, 27
  frequency of, 32
  from a stranger, 30
  Internet, 27-28
  paying and bartering for, 31-32
  preparing for, 23

rhabdomancy, 131

rhapsodomancy, 178

ritual bathing, 42

rituals, spells and, 43-47

rods,
  casting, 143-146
    history of, 143
    homemade system, 144
    interpretive values, 144-146
  dowsing, 132-133
    types of wood, 132
    using, 133

runes, 123-126
    alternative symbols for, 124
    making your own, 123-124
    traditional symbols for, 125

S

sacred space, 45
    invocation to protect, 46-47

scrying, divination by, 187-198
    computer and TV screens
        and, 198
    crystals (crystallomancy)
        and, 188-190
        interpretive values for,
            189-190
    mirrors and, 190-198
        directions for making,
            191-193
        interpretive values for, 197
    various mediums for, 187

smudging, 66, 69

sortilege, 115

spells and rituals, empowering
    43-47
    creating sacred space, 45

spiritual benefits of divination,
    16-17

Squdilatc, 78

stichomancy, 178

stones, casting,
    benefits of, 116
    assembling a set of, 117
    qualities of various, 118-119

symbol board, 81

symbols and pictographs, 199-200
    list of symbology Websites,
        199-200

T

tarot cards, 17, 20-22, 53-55, 57,
    59, 62-63, 99-100, 104-106,
    112, 143

tasseography, 168

tea leaves, reading, 168-172
    interpretive values of, 169-172

tironmancy, 162

tools,
    blessing of, 65
    care and keeping of, 65
    divination and using, 18
    dedication of, 65

trash-to-treasure oracle, 126-127
    possible items to read, 127

trickster spirits, 23

tympania, 78

V

Vedic texts, 41

Victorian language of flowers,
    109-111

vizualization, meditation and, 38

vocalizations, 40

W

water witching, 132

*Woman's Dictionary of
    Symbols and Sacred
    Objects, The*, 200

About the Author

Trish Telesco is a mother of three, wife, chief human to five pets, and a full-time professional author with numerous books on the market. These include the best-selling *Exploring Candle Magick, Money Magick, An Enchanted Life, Gardening With the Goddess, A Witch's Beverages and Brews*, and other diverse titles, each of which represents a different area of spiritual interest for her and her readers.

Trish considers herself a down-to-earth Kitchen Witch whose love of folklore and world-wide customs flavor every one of her spells and rituals. Originally self-trained and self-initiated in Wicca, she later received initiation into the Strega tradition of Italy, which gives form and fullness to the folk magick Trish practices. Her strongest beliefs lie in following personal vision, being tolerant of other traditions, making life an act of worship, and being creative so that magick grows with you.

Trish travels at least twice a month to give lectures and workshops around the country. She has appeared on several television segments including *Sightings*, on mulicultural divination systems, and *National Geographic*

Today–Solstice Celebrations. All the while, Trish maintains a strong, visible presence in metaphysical journals including Circle Network News, and on the internet through popular sites such as *www.witchvox.com* (festival focus); her interactive home page, *www.loresinger.com*, and yahoo club, *www.groups.yahoo.com/groups/folkmagicwithtrishtelesco*; and various appearances on Internet chats and bbs boards.

Her hobbies include gardening, herbalism, brewing, singing, hand crafts, antique restoration, and landscaping. Her current project is helping support various Neo-Pagan causes, including land funds for religious retreats.

Also by Trish Telesco
From New Page Books

Animal Spirit

A Charmed Life

The Cyber Spellbook

An Enchanted Life

Exploring Candle Magick

Gardening With the Goddess

God/Goddess

Mastering Candle Magick

Money Magick

A Witch's Beverages and Brews